Contents

About the Authors

Sarah Hargreaves

Sarah Hargreaves has 12 years experience of management consultancy, research, writing and training in the public and voluntary sectors with Framework, an independent consultancy group. She offers team development, strategic planning, facilitation, board training and development and, from October 1998, training in managing absence. She is co-author of *Managing Staff For The First Time*. She works with a value base of social equality, empowerment and ethical practice.

Telephone 0116 255 7453.

Christina Morton

Christina Morton is a partner at Sinclair Taylor & Martin Solicitors, and specialises in advising the firm's clients on employment and human resources issues. The firm has been advising charitable and voluntary organisations for almost 20 years. The members of the Charity Team have written and lectured widely on the legal issues affecting the voluntary sector and those who work in partnership with it.

Telephone 0181 969 3667.

Gill Taylor

Gill Taylor MIPD has 17 years of personnel management work and consultancy experience in the voluntary sector. Her specialisms are: Training on managing people, managing conflict, managing absence; Facilitating difficult team situations; Consultancy on discipline and dismissal, managing conflict and creating effective organisation structures and employment strategies; Job evaluation and salary structure reviews. Gill has written eight publications on management.

Telephone 0116 270 5876.

Training Courses on Managing Absence

The authors have developed a one and two-day training module on Managing Absence that can be adapted with examples and resources specifically tailored for the:

- voluntary sector;
- health sector;
- education sector; and
- other public service departments.

Please get in touch with any of the authors to discuss the training modules.

Foreword

In my capacity as a Human Resources advisor to the voluntary sector I receive many calls concerning human resources and employment practices. Near the top of the list of questions I am asked is how to manage absence. It can be an area where similar organisations often do not have written procedures. Even large organisations may not have written guidelines for managers. It is in these circumstances that mistakes can easily happen and consistency becomes impossible.

In the past poor management in the area of absence has been overlooked by organisations in all sectors sometimes causing misunderstanding and bad relations between staff and management. Costs are often higher than realised, particularly when those relating to the additional resources needed to cover for paid or unpaid absence or the stress caused when one member of the team is away for long periods is taken into account.

There is an increasing and continuing call for all organisations to become more professional in their approach to employment practice. This is particularly true of voluntary organisations who often, and understandably, focus intently on their users or clients and leave employment policies a long way down the list of priorities. With the increase in employment legislation and the need for highly motivated employees in all sectors of business, employers need well formulated policies and practices to assist delivery of their business goals.

Managing Absence is a comprehensive guide to all types of absence; in addition it gives examples of policies and procedures in this area and an analysis of the implications of new European legislation on employment that affects management of absence. It should also be remembered that UK legislation in the area of absence is already complex. For instance, tribunal findings from the Disability Discrimination Act 1995 are only just beginning to assist employment advisors to interpret the law.

Clarity in management practice in this area is much needed and *Managing Absence* gives direction on how to formulate sound policy statements and management guidelines, ranging from stress related illnesses, long term sickness to the definition of disabled under the Disability Discrimination Act 1995.

As the idea of more flexibility towards working hours and responsibilities of employees outside the workplace grows, this area of managing absence will grow in importance to all sizes of organisations. European legislation has been leading the UK along this path for some time but it is in line with thinking in the UK on discrimination and perhaps highlights a more diverse approach to work itself. I intend to keep this book by me when at work. It will give me a framework for offering advice to employers on legislation and a structure to inform my thinking on employment practices.

Joy Dyson
National Council for Voluntary Organisations, 1998

CN 658.3122
AN 95233

MANAGING ABSENCE

A Handbook for Managers in Public and Voluntary Organisations

Sarah Hargreaves,
Christina Morton
and Gill Taylor

Russell House

Northern College
Library

NC06901

N COLLEGE LIBRARY

BARNSLEY S75 3ET

CANCELLED

First published in 1998 by

Russell House Publishing Limited
4 St. George's House
Uplyme Road Business Park
Lyme Regis
Dorset
DT7 3LS

© Sarah Hargreaves, Christina Morton and Gill Taylor

All rights reserved. No part of this publication may be reproduced, stored in a retrieval system or transmitted in any form, or by any means, electronic, mechanical, photocopying, recording or otherwise, without the prior permission of the Copyright owner or the publisher.

British Library Cataloguing-in-Publication data:
A catalogue record for this book is available from the British Library.

ISBN: 1-898924-17-1

Typeset by Interleaf Productions Limited, Sheffield
Printed by Short Run Press, Exeter

Introduction

Typical queries about absence

'Is there a reasonable attendance level that I can expect from staff?'

'What rights do staff have to maternity and holiday absence?'

'Can I get sick pay back for every day off?'

'How many staff should I reasonably budget for not to put undue strain on the others? What if the health authority won't accept my figures?'

'Sumita has broken her leg and won't be back for about three months. How can we afford a locum if we have to pay her sick pay?'

'Does Tyrone really need all those days off because his children are sick? What's reasonable to expect?'

'How can I tell if someone is not telling the truth about their days off?'

'We can't carry a high level of absence, so can I sack someone fairly for being off with different illnesses over a six-month period?'

'We suspended someone for gross misconduct and now she's gone off sick. What can we do?'

'Why is Pippa off sick for every staff meeting? If no one is doing anything about it, why can't I be off sick for every staff meeting?'

'Where can we get long term sickness insurance cover?'

The above questions are some of the many that managers have about absence. This book aims to explore the legal and management issues in providing the answers to them. We hope that it will be used to ensure that managers are confident about managing absence of all kinds and are confident that staff attendance can be at its optimum for the organisation.

This book is for senior and middle managers working in voluntary and public sector organisations. It aims to meet the needs of the more experienced personnel specialist in a larger organisation as well as the needs of a senior manager in a smaller organisation who may be unfamiliar with unusual absence issues. The book is also for employees at all levels requiring more information.

The main issues explored are:

- common strategic management issues;
- employees' and employers' legal rights and responsibilities;
- statutory rights to time off;
- common contractual absences;
- how to judge the balance of acceptable and unacceptable levels of absence;
- what to do if sickness levels become unacceptable and how to respond fairly;
- making financial provision to safeguard service delivery and other employees when staff are absent.

How to use the book

We suggest you read chapters 1, 2 and 3 which cover management and legal framework and the rights of atypical workers respectively – and then refer to the section of interest.

The Resource section at the back of this book, provides pointers for further investigation and sources of further advice.

The legal position described in the text is the same in Scotland. It is up to date to 31/12/97.

Volunteers

The position of volunteers is not covered in this book. The legal and management framework as described, applies to employees only.

Examples

We have included examples in most of the chapters of the book. We have taken them from those collected by us and acknowledged at the beginning. A range of these examples is given to provide the reader with a picture of what other organisations do. Inclusion does not necessarily mean that in our view it is good practice.

National Joint Council (NJC)

The National Joint Council (NJC) represents local authority staff in the UK and their employees (other than those for whom there are alternative arrangements) and other authorities of equivalent status. Its principal role is to reach agreement, based on shared values, on a national scheme of pay and conditions for local application throughout the UK. The new national agreement from 1 April 1997 for the former Associated Professional, Technical and Clerical (APT&C) staff and manual employees will consist of a new handbook to be known as the *Green Book*. This replaces the previous *APT&C Purple Book* and the *Manual Handbook*. It is referred to throughout in the examples of contract clauses concerning absence.

Acknowledgements

Copyright permissions

First of all a special thanks to Income Data Services for allowing us to use information from their recent study on parental leave in chapter 8 and their study on discretionary leave in Chapter 9. Also to the Child Poverty Action Group for use of information from the *Rights Guide to Non-Means-Tested Benefits* 1997/98 in the section on Statutory Sick Pay in Chapter 5.

Suppliers of information

In addition we have relied greatly on information given to us in confidence by many voluntary and public organisations. With many thanks for your support to: Anna Barclay, Office Manager, Glasgow Association for Mental Health; Ella Bennett, Human Resources Manager and Alison Cobb, Policy Officer, MIND; Doug Bourn, Director, Development Education Association; Chris Butler, Senior Secretary Resources, National Youth Agency; Deborah Cooper, Director, SKILL; National Bureau for Students with Disabilities; Howard Day, Principal Youth Officer, London Borough of Richmond-upon-Thames; Joy Dyson, Human Resources Advisor, National Council of Voluntary Organisations; Employers' Forum on Disability; Richard Excel, TUC; Friends Provident Life Office; Kerris Fryer, Norwich Union Healthcare; Simon Fuchs, London Lighthouse; Lesley Greenaway, Volunteer Development Scotland; Rod Hunter, SHARE, Glasgow; Sam Maher, Human Resources Adviser, and Chris Gerske, Head of Human Resources, Leicester City Council; Moira Halliday, Framework; Rachel Hurst, Disability Awareness in Action; Mary Maybin, Framework; Val McCarthy, Education Department, Leicester City Council; Mo Murray, Manager, Care and Repair (West Leicestershire) Ltd; Teresa O'Neill, Personnel Director, Bryson House; Shirley Otto, Independent Consultant, Edinburgh; Jacqui Parfitt, Marketing Department, Legal and General; Helen Pearson, Henry Moore Sculpture Trust; Tim Pickles, Framework; Penny Sharland, Framework; Jo Verrent, Director, East Midlands Shape; Nicky Wilkins, Director, Care and Repair; and Sally Witcher, Director, Child Poverty Action Group.

Readers

The following readers aided us greatly by commenting on the nearly finished text and allowing us to ensure its accuracy and usefulness: Joy Dyson, Human Resources Advisor, National Council for Voluntary Organisations who also wrote the Foreword; James Sinclair Taylor and colleagues at Sinclair Taylor & Martin; Paul Ticher, Information Management Consultant; and Jo Verrent, Director of East Midlands Shape.

The mistakes remain all our own!

This book has been aided in production by the support of our partners, Chris Housden, Aubrey Kurlansky and Paul Ticher both directly and indirectly, and the tolerance of our children, Shey and Rowan, Laura and Francesca and Sophie and Bridget.

Indemnity: This book is not a full statement of the law, nor does it reflect changes after 31 December 1997 with a few exceptions. It is intended for guidance only and is not a substitute for professional advice. No responsibility for loss occasioned as a result of any person acting or refraining from acting can be accepted by the publisher or the authors.

List of Abbreviations

ACAS	Advisory, Conciliation and Arbitration Service
CRE	Commission for Racial Equality
DDA	Disability Discrimination Act 1995
EAT	Employment Appeals Tribunal
ECJ	European Court of Justice
EOC	Equal Opportunities Commission
EP(C)A	Employment Protection (Consolidation) Act 1978
EqPA	Equal Pay Act 1970
ERA	Employment Rights Act 1996
ET	Employment Tribunal
EU	European Union
EWC	Expected Week of Confinement
HSC	Health and Safety Council
HSE	Health and Safety Executive
HSWA	Health and Safety at Work Act 1974
MSP	Medical Suspension Pay
NIC	National Insurance Contribution
NJC	National Joint Council
OHS	Occupational Health Service
PHI	Permanent Health Insurance
RRA	Race Relations Act 1976
SDA	Sex Discrimination Act 1975
SI	Statutory Instrument
SMP	Statutory Maternity Pay
SSA	Social Security Acts 1986 and 1989
SSCBA	Social Security Contributions and Benefits Act 1992
SSHBA	Social Security and Housing Benefits Acts 1982 and 1983
SSP	Statutory Sick Pay
TUC	Trade Union Congress
TULR(C)A	Trade Unions and Labour Relations Consolidation Act 1992
TUPE	Transfer of Undertakings and Protection of Employment Regulations 1981
TURERA	Trade Union Reform and Employment Rights Act 1993
VDU	Visual Display Unit
WA	Wages Act 1986
WTD	Working Time Directive

Chapter One

Management Framework

Some issues are common to all organisations and cut across absence management. These are explored generally in this section and highlighted as necessary chapter by chapter.

1.1 General approach to absence management

All employees need to be absent from work occasionally, for example:

- a dentist's appointment;
- sudden sickness of the childminder;
- waiting in for the plumber;
- attending a funeral;
- being ill.

Some absences are allowed for in law as statutory rights – there can be no argument about them. They must be in the contract and given to staff in writing. Examples include:

- attendance at ante natal clinics;
- maternity;
- regular attendance at dialysis clinic;
- public service.

Some absences are given in the specific contract an employee has with their employer, for example:

- holiday allowances;
- arrangements for taking time off in lieu;
- maternity leave in addition to statutory provision;
- paternity leave;
- annual attendance at health screening or blood donor clinics.

Organisations will always have some degree of staff absence for illness and other reasons

A certain level of absence is inevitable.
A certain level becomes regarded as normal and may be used in planning staffing levels.
A certain level is acceptable in law.
A certain level is acceptable in the contract.

Then a certain level becomes unacceptable.

As we can see, the issue is more complex than many managers appreciate at first glance. A successful policy on absenteeism is likely to be one that takes account of the details behind the absence statistics and of individual circumstances. It will take health promotion and health and safety measures seriously. It will keep under review a wide range of employment policies including those on leave arrangements and working conditions.

Employers need to acknowledge the wider context that may be affecting absence rates. Policies need to be flexible rather than mechanistic and geared towards individuals' circumstances, whilst ensuring consistent treatment of different members of staff. It is an organisational responsibility to ensure low absence as well as the employee's.

If any staff member can't work because of absence, a balance has to be struck between their need for time to recover to full health or to deal with other personal issues or commitments and the organisation's need for services to be provided efficiently and for staff morale to be maintained. In our view this is the essence of good practice in managing absence.

1.2 Absence Statistics

Far more working days are lost each year in Britain through absence than through strikes. A survey in 1994 by the Trades Union Congress and Labour Research Department found that across 83 workplaces the average absence rate was 4.8 per cent, but this varied between departments, types of work and from week to week. All statistics quoted concern absence for sickness and absence for other unauthorised reasons. That is it does not include holidays and absences for other contractual rights.

Examples of absence statistics

- A Confederation of British Industry survey in 1993 found that 3.5 per cent of working time was lost to sickness at a cost to employers of £13 billion per year. This gives an average of eight days per annum/per employee. The rate for manual workers was twice that of non-manual staff. They also found that the average absence rate varies from 2.0 to 5.1 per cent, depending on different industrial sectors.

- The Labour Force Survey of 1994 shows variations by industry: Distribution, hotels, restaurants, banking and finance had an absence rate of just under four per cent. Public administration, education and health had a rate of five per cent. Other industries ranked in between. Where data is available it shows that absence rates in the public sector are 40 per cent higher than in the private sector (People Management). By occupation, managers and administrators were on three per cent and manual operatives on 5.5 per cent, with other occupations ranked in between. (Labour Research Department publication on Sick Pay, February 1995.)

- A recent survey on flexible working and absence rates shows that the national norm is 3.59 per cent whereas organisations with flexible working hours reported a rate of 3.13 per cent. (Industrial Society Report.)

- A National Audit Office report in 1997 found that sickness absence is costing the police force in England and Wales 1.5 million working days and £210 million per annum. For the Metropolitan police the cost is £88 million and almost 400,000 working days per year. The Metropolitan police's rate of 14.4 days sickness absence per year was higher than the national average. Between 16 and 77 per cent of the officers in any one force were taking early retirement on medical grounds.

- Research undertaken by Dr Melvin Kettle of the University of Bradford for the Association of Disabled Professionals shows that 72.6 per cent of disabled employees had work production rates as good as or higher than non-disabled employees. They had fewer injuries and were absent for fewer days per injury.

- There are no specific figures associated with the voluntary sector. A reasonable working figure would seem to be to allow for 3.6 per cent for absences including sickness but not including holidays, when planning staffing levels.

1.3 Statutory rights and responsibilities

The law sets out a framework of employee's rights and employer's responsibilities in the area of absence from work. Some of these are statutory rights, for example time off for union activities. Rights may be specifically written out in documents deemed to have contractual status, for example the statement of particulars, the staff handbook or the letter of appointment. Others are called implied terms – ones that exist without needing to be written down. The primary implied term in relation to absence is the employers' duty of care.

1.3.1 Employers' duties

Employers' have a responsibility in law to take reasonable care for the safety of employees. Staff must not be put in undue danger of accident or contracting illnesses through their work. Employers also have a duty of care. This means not placing staff in a position to damage their health through excessive or dangerous duties.

Managers have responsibilities to make sure that the service is delivered. They also have delegated responsibilities on behalf of an employing body to ensure that the staff are not put under undue stress or asked to carry workloads that are detrimental to their health. Committees and senior managers should be aware of this responsibility when planning staffing levels or work rotas.

1.3.2 Employees' duties and rights

Duties. Employees also have implied duties. The main ones in relation to absence are: the duty to exercise care in the performance of their duties, and the duty to obey lawful and reasonable instructions.

Rights. When dealing with absence it is important not to start from a position that the staff are always in the wrong – or causing difficulties for the organisation. The law relating to absence from work raises the following issues in particular:

- the right to a healthy and safe working environment. Absence may become an issue if an employee becomes sick or lacking in motivation because of poor working conditions or stress arising from poor management;
- the statutory rights to absence on the grounds set out in the employment legislation;
- the rights of employees who are sick;
- the rights of absent employees to payment and levels of pay entitlement;
- the rights of particular groups of employees such as pregnant workers and employees with disabilities;
- whether and in what circumstances an employer is entitled to dismiss an employee on account of absence for sickness or other reason.

On the other hand, where there are situations where rights are being abused, managers have the right to take firm action.

1.3.3 Legal summary

Legal framework

The legal framework is made up of:

- UK statutes and statutory instruments, in particular:
- Health and safety legislation, mainly the Health and Safety at Work Act 1974, the Management of Health and Safety at Work Regulations 1992 and the Health and Safety (Consultation with Employees) Regulations 1996.
- Employment legislation, mainly the Employment Rights Act 1996.
- Equal opportunities legislation – the Sex Discrimination Act 1975, the Race Relations Act 1976 and the Disability Discrimination Act 1995.

- Trade union legislation – the Trade Union and Labour Relations (Consolidation) Act 1992.
- The rules for Statutory Maternity Pay and Statutory Sick Pay contained in the Social Security Contributions and Benefits Act 1992 and the Social Security Administration Act 1992.
- The law on access to information about employees health – the Access to Medical Reports Act 1988 and the Access to Medical Records Act 1990.
- European law, in particular the Directives on Working Time; the rights of Part-time and Atypical Workers and Parental Leave.
- Rights under the contract of employment and at common law including implied and expressed terms.

1.4 Organisations and culture

All workplaces have a culture of acceptable and unacceptable behaviour, regardless of the legal parameters for action. Organisational culture is often hard to define and make explicit. Culture operates in relation to all aspects of being at work including: dress codes; acceptable language; acceptability of management action; expectations about staff adherence to the value system expressed in the mission statement; how much information the employing body is given and so on.

1.4.1 Culture

The particular culture in an organisation is individual to that particular organisation. It is one of the main things a new employee will try to find out about as soon as possible. It is one of the reasons we talk about the 'feel' of an organisation or team. For example, there may be a culture that insists on people being seen to be at work and not leaving at the end of the day before the senior manager leaves. Culture can vary across different departments or locations in the same organisation regardless of written policy. In fact, in some organisations written policies are kept in the dusty drawer and bear no relation to what actually happens in teams. This itself is a feature of an organisation's culture.

Understanding the culture operating in your organisation in relation to absence is important. Your understanding of it will influence how you go about changing it and may explain some reactions from staff if you are trying to introduce a more 'managed' environment.

Broad cultural themes

Some broad cultural themes that influence the attitudes towards absence are:

How acceptable 'close' management is

Staff can have the attitude that monitoring their timekeeping is in effect policing. This can be expressed as follows:

> Insisting I fill my timesheet in every day suggests that you are policing my every move. Wanting to know where I am at all times is unacceptable. So I won't fill in the diary, remember to tell the receptionist where I am, call in after every client appointment, push the in/out slide across my name rigorously etc..

How much the organisation gives staff the freedom to manage themselves

Some staff may take advantage of loose or non-existent management monitoring. This can be related to the attitude above.

> I manage my own time and work out when I need to get to appointments. If I take a bit of spare time to go shopping that's my business. I give a lot back in spare overtime hours that I never claim for. It shows a lack of trust in me and my truthfulness to have to account for my whereabouts all day. Why can't you trust me to be responsible according to my own standards?

Expectations about commitment to the organisation

Staff in the voluntary sector often engage in self-exploitation. They work overtime and don't take off all the time off in lieu they are owed. A common unspoken trade-off is that:

> I'll work hard for you and not claim all my TOIL, but I don't want to be closely scrutinised in my timekeeping and monitored about my whereabouts every moment of the day. I also reserve the right to take a long lunch break as it suits me at the last moment.

Taking holidays

Some staff may feel that they work so hard or give so much time to the organisation that they should be allowed holidays exactly when they want and for as long as they want.

> I work very hard for you and I want to have three weeks off when I want them at short notice. I don't want to have to negotiate about cover or fit in with the school holidays. I have a right to take my holidays when I want them.

The broad cultural background to an organisation affects how issues that come up time and again in relation to sickness and absences are treated. The standard management reaction will be different for each organisation, and tends to run along a continuum. Roughly the continuum goes from hard-line close management to lax management. Five examples follow.

Sickness absence examples

See if you can recognise where your organisation fits in each example. Is stated policy different from what really happens?

What you can be off sick for

> Never * At death's door * Broken leg * Acute food poisoning * Period pains * Headache * Feeling off

Whether it is intrusive to ask about sickness absences

> Return to work interview every time * Monitor only if over a certain number of days * Casual chat: Are you alright? * Not mention it

Reporting absences

> By nine am without fail or lose a day's pay * By nine am to office or to line manager as far as is possible * Sometime in the morning * Sometime during the day * Not bothered

Accounting for whereabouts

> Not saying where you are consistently is an automatic disciplinary offence * Certain standards expected and monitored * Lax about monitoring * Other staff lucky to know if someone is in the building or not

Timekeeping

> Timesheet filled in every day meticulously to last quarter hour * Timesheets filled in once a week approximately * Holidays and TOIL noted on a record sheet somewhere for pay purposes * Timesheet? What's that?

Entitlement to time off for being ill. Another common cultural issue is that staff in some organisations come to an idea that a certain number of days' sickness can be taken off **as of right** on top of annual leave. This arises from the reasonable idea that a certain number of days off for illness each year is acceptable. However, in some organisations where this attitude goes unchallenged absence rates can rise as high as 15 per cent. This is clearly unacceptable and leads to problems in managing service delivery.

1.4.2 Maintaining flexibility

When managing absence, it is important to have some leeway for taking into consideration different people and their wellness or level of commitments outside work. The common boundaries for action should still stand. If you have staff working flexible hours, or working from home, or travelling a lot you will need good systems for monitoring, recording and managing absence.

1.5 Strategic management issues

1.5.1 What affects attendance levels?

Getting good attendance is a complex management skill. There are many factors to take into account. Staff may feel they do not get enough holiday time and so take it anyway as sick leave. Behind even genuine sickness can be a feeling of boredom and a lack of motivation. Low absenteeism often shows that staff really want to come to work.

Management factors affecting attendance

The main factors that need to be taken into account are:

Factor	Consequence
Poor planning of staffing levels	Institutionalised overload Burnout
Unrealistic costing of staffing levels	High turnover of staff Waste of resources
Poor design of jobs	
No policy on legitimate absences	Inconsistent management action
Lack of health and safety standards Lack of health promotion	Unnecessary risks to health
Poor management performance/bullying culture	Low staff morale. Poor work boundaries
Lack of capability	Inefficient use of resources
Lack of management information on absence	Ineffectiveness and inconsistency

---

What to do about these main causes of absence is discussed in brief in the following sections.

Motivation. Staff motivation can play a part in absence levels. If people really don't want to be at work, colds can turn into flu and Monday-morning-itis into a day in bed. While nearly all staff take the odd day off occasionally, this sort of absence can soon mount up to a significantly increased absence level. If a supervision session picks up a lack of motivation, try and tackle it as a management issue before it causes further problems. Find out about the causes of it – such as poor job design, boredom, difficulties in the team, lack of training, personal development needs – and try to address them with the employee. There may be a stress related reason for poor motivation. See Chapter 5.

1.5.2 Strategy and planning staffing structure

Absence is only one of the issues of personnel management. It is related to other key management functions. These have to be understood at a strategic level before they are dealt with at line manager level. At a strategic level this is about costing staff time properly and planning posts and levels of responsibilities that are congruent. This must not inevitably lead to overload regardless of the level of competence of the post holder.

Costing staff levels. When staff levels are planned to ensure service delivery within budgets or in funding bids, managers do not usually consistently budget for absence. There can be an unwritten expectation that managers want workers to be at work all the time – regardless of personal needs or health issues.

Costing staffing example

One example comes from the nursing profession (quoted in *Getting Organised, A Handbook for Non-statutory Organisations*):

If one patient requires between one and one-and-a-half nurses

Ten patients need	Minimum	Maximum
Ten baseline workers	10	15
Allowances for absence 5%	10.5	15.75
Allowances for holidays 10%	11.5	17.25
Allowances for maternity and other statutory leave 2%	11.73	17.55
Allowances for extra work in small units of under 30 patients of 2% per patient (max 20%)	14.08	19.55
Total workers required	15	20

Whatever your organisation's way of costing staffing levels don't forget to include a percentage for training courses, sickness absence, holidays and other statutory absences. There is also usually a time-lag between one worker leaving and a new worker starting in post. Where the service cannot be suspended, locum cover or extra hours from other staff may need to be arranged.

When collecting statistics about sickness absence it is important to make distinctions between absence for short term reasons, long term ill health and predictable absences for a known recurrent health problem. There are well documented factors making some categories of employees more or less prone to having time off work: manual workers take more time than non-manual workers; women's absence rates are higher; there are also variations by age and across different sectors.

Job design. Not many organisations feel they have the luxury of enough time to carry out a full job analysis each time they write a job description. However, it can be beneficial to much of the future success of the job. Good written material provides a sound basis for efficient management of services, useful appraisal of review sessions and effective supervision for both the postholder and their manager. Obviously, how a job description is carried out is open to interpretation and jobs do develop, but getting the job description right is essential to avoid as much future conflict as possible.

Avoiding mistakes in job design. Many job descriptions come about through:
- organic development of what the employing body thinks needs doing;
- what the previous job holder was good at and saw as important;
- a hodge-podge of what the out-going job holder did and other people don't want to do;
- developing from what a volunteer was doing;
- deriving from project aims that got funded, but are tacked onto the main organisation;
- being copied from another organisation;
- a generic collective duties description;
- being handed down from a similar organisation or department;
- it seemed like a good idea at the time.

All of these sources have their problems!

Lack of clarity in a job description may lead to:

- discipline and grievance problems – Employment Tribunal at worst;
- lack of clear direction for the organisation;
- team problems over different interpretation of job descriptions or the importance of the various tasks within the job description;

When you are designing jobs do not:

- Use the same old job description for the next job holder unless you're sure it is still right for the job.
- Create a job description out of the bits of work no one else wants to do. (This will lead to an impossible job which will have a high staff turnover and/or high staff stress level. Either of these will be costly in terms of management time, staff time, and general unhappiness at work.)
- Mix radically different skill areas in one job description such as finance and fundraising or personnel and computer manager.

When designing posts do take into account the following:

- the aim and purpose of the job;
- the tasks that need doing;
- the relationship to other jobs in the organisation;
- how it fits in with the organisation's priorities;
- what sort of support the job gets from or gives to other staff.

Managing staff levels. Posts may be vacant for some time if there is a funding crisis or when staff leave suddenly, leave with short notice periods, or fail to return from a sabbatical. In this case the work priorities must be shifted for remaining staff so that they are not expected to do the work of the missing post on top of their own work. They must also be involved in any discussion about the new arrangements. Covering for the absence of crucial employees might be handled by a junior person acting up or by locum cover. Any employee acting up will need more management support than a fully qualified and trained post holder. They should also be paid at an appropriately increased salary scale.

1.5.3 Policies on absence

It is vital to clarify statutory rights and any additional contractual rights to absence. If the contract is unclear or does not mention statutory rights, this can lead to resentments on the part of staff. Where contract clauses are vague, clarify and ensure consistent management implementation. For larger employers it is worth considering a policy and a special guidance document for middle managers who have to implement the policy.

1.5.4 Health and safety and health promotion

Health and safety is a big issue in all sectors. The voluntary sector is particularly poor at taking responsibilities seriously, often asking employees to work in very unsuitable, cramped or potentially dangerous conditions. Even if these are not affecting immediate performance or motivation they can potentially lead to long term health problems.

1.5.5 Poor performance of managers

When you have a good picture of absence in an organisation, you may find a pattern emerging. For example, one particular team or department may have a significantly higher level than other parts of the organisation. This may be a clue to potential poor performance; either because of lack of capability of an employee or a manager. For example, if a secretarial or assistant post has a high turnover of staff, it will be legitimate to ask about the management style of the manager of that employee. If you do uncover bullying or harassment as a result of this, always take action. Failure to do so will potentially result in huge penalties from an Employment Tribunal should any of the employees take formal action.

A TUC hotline set up for the first five days of December 1997, found that 38 per cent of the calls were about bullying, 25 per cent about pay, 15 per cent about breach of contract, 13 per cent about long hours, 11 per cent about dismissal and 11 per cent about health and safety. A quarter of callers were managers and professionals, a lot of whom complained of bullying from their own managers.

1.5.6 What managers should do

One possible **action programme** for managers concerned about absence would be the following:

1. Get information: ensure that managers know what the absences rates are in the organisation and have a detailed break down by team or department.
    You need information which can be:
    *   analysed by reason for the absence;
    *   retrieved by individual;
    *   analysed to give overall team, department and organisation percentages.

2. Set up absence reporting mechanisms:
    *   ensure timesheets are properly filled in and monitored;
    *   design a system for reporting absence including a requirement for staff to clear it in advance when appropriate;
    *   decide when to take action on absence, set up return to work interviews and train managers to deal with absence.

3. Find out reasons for poor performance/poor attendance record. (Take action on any organisational factors before blaming the employee.)

4. Clarify statutory rights and contractual rights to absence: (Chapters 4 and 8)
    *   get these written into the contract;
    *   provide guidance to staff if necessary;
    *   use codes of practice where appropriate.

5. Develop a sickness absence policy, train on it, implement it and monitor it (Chapter 5).

6. Ensure good job design and staffing level planning mechanisms are in the business or forward plan.

7. Carry out health and safety risk assessments properly and do something about the risks (Chapters 3 and 5).

8. Consider insurance for staff sickness – at least decide if it is worth it (Chapter 10).

9. Keep confidentiality about individual employees' health issues and other reasons for absence throughout the organisation.

Chapter Two

Legal Framework

2.1 UK statutes and statutory instruments

This is a legal framework and in some places it points you to the main legislation.

2.1.1 Health and safety legislation

All employers are required to ensure as far as is reasonably practicable the health and safety of their employees at work. Compliance with health and safety legislation will almost certainly bring about a reduction in the number of likely absences in a particular workplace. The employer's duty encompasses:

- the place of work, including means of access to and exit from it;
- the equipment, appliances and plant within the workplace;
- the system under which the work is carried out.

The 1974 Health and Safety at Work Act provides the framework under which regulations are brought in from time to time. A number were brought in in 1992 and there have been some further regulations since. Under the 1992 Regulations the employer is under a duty to carry out a hazard analysis of the workplace in order to identify and manage risks.

Employers and health and safety

The law imposes a clear duty on employers to assess risks, inform staff and keep up to date with the law. Employers must:

- appoint a competent person to carry out risk assessment;
- put in place adequate preventative and protective measures to guard against identified risks;
- ensure that all employees, temporary or permanent, receive proper instruction, training and supervision and are kept fully informed of risks which might affect them and of the steps they can take to minimise and eliminate those risks;
- put in place proper arrangements for the use, handling, storage and transport of the employer's goods;
- ensure that machinery and equipment is fit for the purpose, properly cleaned and maintained and safe to use;
- co-operate with others sharing the workplace in the discharge of the various health and safety obligations;
- record, if there are five or more employees, significant findings of the risk assessments and preventative measures;
- keep abreast of developing knowledge.

An employer's duty is to the particular employee. Individual characteristics and the needs of the individual must be taken into account when assessing risks.

Employees also have health and safety obligations. These include:

- taking care of their own health and safety and that of their colleagues;

- co-operating with the employer on health and safety issues;

- using equipment only in accordance with the instructions and training which they have received;

- informing the employer of any work situation which in their opinion constitutes 'a serious and imminent danger' or of any shortcomings in the employer's arrangements for health and safety (see also Chapter 5, Section 2).

2.1.2 Employment legislation

The main statute is now the Employment Rights Act 1996 (ERA) which consolidated the Employment Protection (Consolidation) Act 1978, the Wages Act 1986, parts of the Trade Union Reform and Employment Rights Act 1993 and miscellaneous other laws. In relation to absence from work the ERA covers most of the statutory rights to time off. These are covered in detail in Chapters 4 and 8.

The law on unfair dismissal. The ERA also sets out the basis of the law on unfair dismissal. The law has been greatly amplified and developed by case law but the basic framework is in the act. The ERA allows an employer to dismiss an employee who qualifies for statutory protection from unfair dismissal:

- if the employer can establish one of the statutory grounds for dismissal; and

- if the employer acts reasonably in treating the circumstances which led to dismissal as grounds for dismissal (the courts have interpreted this as implying the necessity to follow a fair and reasonable procedure).

Statutory grounds for dismissal. A reason for dismissal is allowed by S98 of the ERA if:

- it relates to the capability or qualifications of the employee for performing the work of the kind the employee was employed to do;

- it relates to the conduct of the employee;

- the employee is redundant;

- the employee could not continue to work without contravention of a statutory enactment;

- the employer has some other substantial reason which would justify dismissal.

The employer is required to act reasonably both in treating the reason as a reason for dismissal and in the dismissal procedures the employer adopts.

The law on dismissal and absence management. This is relevant to the issues of absence management mainly in two ways.

First, if an employee is abusing a statutory or contractual right to time off from work this is a matter of the employee's conduct and may lead to disciplinary proceedings which culminate in dismissal. Misconduct is one of the potentially fair grounds for dismissal under the ERA.

Secondly, if an employee's absence through sickness, disability or stress becomes, through its frequency or duration, intolerable for the employer, then this may raise a question of the employee's capability to carry out the work they were employed to do. Lack of capability is also potentially a fair ground for dismissal.

Some cases of persistent short term absence do not in fact raise issues of the employee's capability because they all relate to separate complaints rather than to one underlying disabling condition. If they become unsustainable for the employer then the reason for dismissal would fall into the category of 'some other substantial reason justifying dismissal'. In either case the assessment the employer makes of the facts and the procedure the employer adopts are crucial.

Chapter 4 looks at statutory rights to time off and covers briefly the parameters of employers' action when these are abused. Chapter 5 looks in detail at the procedures an employer must adopt in order to dismiss an employee fairly when the employee's capability to do the job is in question.

Employers also need to be aware that the ERA gives some employees protection from unfair dismissal no matter how long they have been employed i.e. no qualifying period applies. This includes pregnant women – dismissal for a reason connected with pregnancy is automatically unfair regardless of length of service. This is also the case for dismissal for taking time off where the employee has a statutory right (see Chapters 4 and 8).

2.1.3 Equal opportunities legislation

Employers must not treat different members of staff inconsistently in the way they respond to and manage absence issues. The reasons for this include:

- the likelihood of causing resentment;
- the likelihood of lowering morale;
- the possibility of claims of sex, race or disability discrimination if it seemed that one sex or one ethnic group or employees with disabilities were being treated less favourably than others.

Imposing a requirement or condition which it is harder for a particular group to meet can amount to indirect discrimination. It is particularly an issue for women employees who want to work reduced or flexible hours although it is open to an employer to argue that indirect sex or race discrimination is justified (see Chapter 3).

Employers have an additional duty to disabled employees to consider reasonable adjustments in the workplace which might well include adjustments to working hours or other measures, which could have an impact on the time a disabled employee is actually present at work. Employers might be able to justify differences of treatment of disabled staff. The issues are considered in detail in Chapter 7.

2.1.4 Trade Union legislation

The TULR(C)A 1992 sets out the right of trade union representatives to time off in connection with their union duties and the rights of trade union members to time off to participate in trade union activities (see Chapter 4).

2.1.5 Statutory Maternity Pay (SMP) and Statutory Sick Pay (SSP)

The rules for the payment and administration of SMP and SSP are set out in the SSCBA 1992 and the Social Security Administration Act 1992 (see Chapter 5 for SSP and chapter 8 for SMP).

2.1.6 Medical reports

Managers dealing with sickness absence will have to comply with the Access to Medical Reports Act 1988. This gives an employee extensive rights. These include the right to:

- refuse permission to the employer to obtain a medical report;
- amend any report obtained;
- deny access to the employer to any report they have commissioned.

Employers may also be able to use the Access to Medical Records Act 1990 which give them wide access to employees' health records with employees' prior consent (see Chapter 5).

2.2 European law

Since the UK signed the Treaty of Rome, European law has become part of the legal framework in the UK. European Directives are binding on the member states of the EC and must be incorporated into the laws of each country.

European law has had a particularly marked impact on employment and health and safety law. Many of the recent changes in UK employment and health and safety law which relate to absence from work have had a European origin, including the changes to maternity rights in 1994 (see Chapter 8) and the Directive on Working Time (see Chapter 6).

The agreement of the UK to sign up to the Social Chapter will also compel the incorporation of the European Directives on parental leave and the rights of part-time workers into UK law (see Chapters 3 and 8).

2.3 Rights under the contract of employment

2.3.1 Express contractual terms

Rights under a contract are sometimes also referred to by lawyers as common law rights. This distinguishes them from statutory rights that are contained in legislation. Some of the terms of an employment contract will have been spelt out either orally or in writing. These are the express terms. There are usually express terms dealing with sickness absence and holidays because the ERA requires it. There may also be other express terms dealing with other kinds of absence such as compassionate leave and carers' leave. The express terms of the contract, whether they are written down or not, must be followed by employers and employees dealing with absence issues.

2.3.2 Implied terms

Both sides must also be aware of implied rights and obligations. These are generally rights and obligations implied into all employment contracts by decisions of the courts and sometimes by statute. Employers, for example, have an implied duty deriving from health and safety legislation to provide a safe system of work and place of work. Employees have an implied duty to carry out their work with reasonable care and skill, among other things.

Periodically the courts extend the list of implied rights and duties. During 1997, for example, the courts said that an employer has an implied duty to investigate promptly any grievance raised by an employee, whatever the issue. They also introduced implied duties in contracts which contain a right to benefits under a permanent health insurance scheme (see Chapter 10).

Acting in contravention of the express or implied terms of an employment contract will leave an employer liable to compensate the employee with damages for the breach. For example, an employer who withholds contractual sick pay from an employee may be liable to pay damages equivalent to the pay which would have been received had the contract been properly carried out by the employer. The employer may leave themselves exposed to further damages if the employee raises a grievance about the employer's handling of the issue but this is not dealt with speedily by the employer.

2.3.3 Frustration of an employment contract

Occasionally events intervene to prevent the performance of an employment contract, for example, the imprisonment of an employee or permanent disablement in an accident. Such an event can sometimes be found to have 'frustrated' the contract so that it comes to an end without the employer or the employee having to take any steps to terminate it. It is difficult for employers to judge whether the circumstances mean that an employment contract has been frustrated by the absence of an employee. It is generally better and safer practice to expressly terminate the contract with proper notice and procedures (see Chapters 4 and 5).

Chapter Three

Atypical Workers

The traditional model of full-time work for a working lifetime is becoming less common. Nevertheless those who do not fit this model are still considered atypical. Changing patterns of work are introducing new challenges for managers and new complexities into the way that existing laws are interpreted and applied by tribunals and courts.

Voluntary and public sector organisations are often at the cutting edge in terms of the arrangements they make with their employees and the flexibility they are prepared to demonstrate. This can leave them vulnerable to uncertainty about how to manage innovative working arrangements. They may also have concerns about how their actions would stand up to legal challenge. This chapter shows how the particular problems for the management of absence raised by varied working patterns can be tackled and considers the legal issues.

Types of workers

Workers may be:

- **permanent full-time:** working full normal working hours for the particular organisation on a permanent contract;

- **permanent part-time:** working on a permanent contract for less than the full normal working hours;

- **fixed-term:** (can be full-time or part-time) working for a fixed period of time between specified dates;

- **temporary:** (can be full or part-time) working for a temporary period that does not have a fixed end date (e.g. a maternity locum);

- **on probation:** (can be any of the above) in an initial period of the contract where different rules may apply to appraisal, dismissal and notice. This is usually dealt with by provisions in the contract of employment which in particular make it clear how long the probationary period will last and whether it can be extended;

- **employed on a zero hours contract:** the individual is clearly an employee but the employer retains complete flexibility as to the number of hours of work offered, which can be no hours at all in some time periods;

- **sessional:** the person works on an 'as and when' basis usually to provide *ad hoc* cover and usually with no guarantee of work or requirement to take work when it is offered. Often used to describe staff in a 'bank' of people available for short term locum cover;

- **casual:** this means different things to different people – anything from what we have described as temporary to what we have called sessional. It has some statutory meaning. The ERA refers to casual staff as those working on contracts of three months or less. The Act denies them the right to statutory notice unless there is a series of contracts which can be strung together to create a period of over three months.

- **self-employed:** working on one's own account and not as an employee. This describes consultants and others providing services to more than one organisation. There are complex tests for self-employment in both employment and tax law. It is often misused where the person concerned would be likely to be considered an employee by a tribunal and/or the Inland Revenue.

- **agency staff:** supplied on a temporary or long term basis by an employment agency – not considered to be an employee of either the agency or the agency's client unless there are specific factors pointing to an employment relationship.

- **seconded staff:** are often employees of another organisation 'lent out' to provide expertise or experience. The terms of the secondment and the responsibility for management of the seconded employee are often left rather vague. This is problematical if conduct or capability issues arise, particularly if disciplinary action looks necessary. It may be unclear which organisation is now the employer and therefore responsible for handling the matter either managerially or in law.

3.1 Why differences in employee status matter

Historically, permanent full-time workers had superior rights to those of the other categories, but this has been changing. In 1994 the government equalised the statutory rights of full and part-time workers following a challenge brought by the Equal Opportunities Commission.

The regulations introduced by the government after its defeat in the House of Lords meant that the old minimum hours thresholds for the acquisition of employment rights were swept away. Previously those working between 8 and 16 hours a week were at a disadvantage, while those working less than eight hours a week never gained most of the important rights.

Since 1994 any employee can gain the full range of statutory employment rights. The change coincided with the extension of maternity rights to all women employees in line with European law (see Chapter 8). Furthermore, the right of part-timers to pro rata terms and conditions has increasingly been recognised as an equality issue. Different treatment of full and part-time workers, in matters such as holidays and sick pay, has formed the basis for potential claims of indirect sex discrimination.

However, as the significance of the distinction between full-timers and part-timers has dwindled the distinction between those whom the law would recognise as employees and those it would not has grown in importance.

3.1.1 The rights of employees compared with non-employees

It is important to make the distinction between employees and non-employees.

Employees have a large number of statutory rights which other categories of workers do not. Many of these are contained in employment protection legislation.
They include:

- the right not to be unfairly dismissed;
- the right to a statutory redundancy payment;
- the right not to have sums unlawfully deducted from wages;
- the right to a statutory minimum notice period;
- the right to take time off work in the circumstances allowed by statute;
- the right to equal pay;
- the right to statutory maternity leave;
- the right not to be dismissed for asserting a statutory right.

There are also wider implications. Among others:

- employers are required to deduct PAYE and NI from employees' pay;
- employers' health and safety obligations to employees and to the self-employed are different;
- employees are entitled to SSP and SMP;
- employees have better protection from discrimination.

3.1.2 The relationship of employee status to absence management

The statutory rights to time off work, discussed in detail in Chapter 4, are only available to employees. Only employees are entitled to maternity leave, SMP and SSP. Only employees are entitled to protection from unfair dismissal and hence to the benefit of proper procedures if their absence from work causes difficulties for the employer. (A worker falling into another category may, however, have a contract which gives similar rights.) It is likely, although not yet entirely clear, that only employees will benefit from future improvements in employment rights such as the statutory right to paid annual holiday and parental leave.

A manager cannot manage employees' absence from work appropriately if the manager does not know which categories of worker have which rights. It is neither possible nor appropriate for employers to play safe by treating everyone as if they have full employment rights. But it can be demoralising for workers to be treated as if they have no rights when in fact they have acquired them. It can be expensive for employers to realise too late that they have made mistakes in the treatment of their staff.

3.2 How to tell who is an employee

This is a difficult question for employers to answer for themselves as the law is changing fast. Legal advice may be necessary. However, here are some examples of people who have been held to have contracts of employment:

- a dentist from private practice who provided emergency cover once a week for a single eight hour shift at the local hospital;
- an agency worker whose contract with the agency contained a contractual grievance procedure and the right of the agency to dismiss the worker for misconduct;
- a person employed to work a five-and-a-half hour shift in a bar once a fortnight;
- a person whose name was kept in a pool of those available for locum cover in a factory, where time spent in the pool was taken into account by the employer in deciding whether to offer permanent positions;
- an employee employed on what her employer described as a 'series of daily contracts', who was found by the court to be eligible for SSP;
- a hotel waitress whose work ceased over the winter months but who was asked by her employer to keep herself available for relief work.

Staff are normally clearly employees if they are permanent (full or part-time) or on one-off fixed term or temporary contracts. It is usually not too difficult to work out their rights. They will have some or all of the statutory rights, depending on their length of service, and any additional rights which are set out in their contracts of employment.

It can be particularly hard to:

- work out the rights of someone who is employed on a casual, sessional or *ad hoc* basis;
- deal with the problem of drift from one legal status to another;
- distinguish between employed and self-employed workers;
- prepare appropriate documentation.

3.2.1 Working out the rights of someone who is employed on a casual, sessional or *ad hoc* basis

There are two key areas: continuity and the presence or absence of an employment relationship.

Continuity issues. Some employment rights depend on continuity. The issue of continuity is the main problem arising for sessional, bank, *ad hoc* locum and casual staff in establishing that they have employment rights which depend on continuity such as the right not to be unfairly dismissed.

Fixed-term and temporary staff who work on more than one contract with the same employer may acquire additional rights. This depends on whether there are any breaks in their contracts of employment. Establishing continuity may be hard. Briefly, continuity is preserved throughout any week in which the employee is under a contract with the employer. However, in some cases the contract survives a break in employment. Deciding where this is the case is a complex question of fact and law. Employers may need advice to sort it out.

There are four situations (S212 of the ERA) in which employment may cease as a result of termination of the contract but continuity is preserved if the contract re-starts within a specified period:

- sickness or injury;
- temporary cessation of work;
- leave of absence under an arrangement or custom;
- pregnancy.

The third situation of preserving continuity under an arrangement or custom can, for example, mean that seasonal staff who return to their employers annually may enjoy continuity of employment notwithstanding seasonal breaks.

Is there an employment relationship? Other important employment rights do not depend on continuity. These include the right to 14 weeks maternity leave and the right not to have unlawful deductions made from wages. Here the issue is whether there is an employment relationship at all. This has often hinged on the question of whether or not there is any 'mutuality of obligation', i.e. is the employer obliged to offer any work and is the employee required to take it?

In clear-cut cases where there is no mutual obligation and no continuity of employment either, the chance of the employee gaining any employment rights is negligible. But there are plenty of cases which fall into a grey area. The difficulties have been made worse by indications from the courts that 'mutuality of obligation' is not a stand-alone test. It can only be considered one factor among many in working out whether a contract of employment exists.

Significantly the EC Directive on Part-Time Work (due to be implemented in the UK by 1999) defines a part-time worker as an employee whose normal hours of work, calculated on a weekly basis or on average over a period of employment of up to one year, are less than the normal hours of work of a comparable full-time worker. This could, if interpreted widely enough, include seasonal and temporary workers.

Member states can opt to exclude from the scope of the Directive part-timers employed on a casual basis, provided there are objective reasons for doing so. 'Casual' is not defined and its meaning differs widely across Europe. It will be up to the member states to work out how an exclusion could work and how wide its scope should be.

3.2.2 The problem of drift from one legal status to another

For some organisations, particularly those working under contracts which require flexibility in planning staffing levels, a further problem is the tendency to drift from one situation to another. For example, a sessional worker might start off doing the odd shift every three or four months. As they build up experience they are gradually asked to do more and more work until they are working several shifts every month, often with less than a week in between shifts. When does such an employee cross the line from sessional with no rights to part-timer with full rights?

Example

One national charity which campaigns on health issues runs a help line on a tightly costed contract from the local health authority. In order to bid competitively for the contract it has to keep staff costs to a minimum. The basic team is supplemented from a bank of sessional staff at annual periods of peak publicity and demand. The sessional staff have basic contracts which contain details of their hourly rates of pay and reference to a Code of Conduct. There is no entitlement to pay for any shift which is not worked, whatever the reason. The service runs in this way for four years. At this point some of the regular sessional workers start to press for clarification of their status. This is triggered by a disciplinary incident following the failure of a sessional worker to attend a pre-arranged shift. There are no procedures in place to deal with issues concerning the conduct or capability of sessional staff. The way in which the disciplinary matter is handled triggers a grievance. When the charity seeks advice as to the sessional worker's right to raise a grievance it transpires that the worker in question has in fact been working five shifts a week for over two years. The ensuing advice is that this worker ought to be treated in the same way as the charity's permanent staff . This triggers a full scale review of the status of the 'sessional' staff. More appropriate contracts and procedures are produced which recognise that a significant proportion of them have continuity of service over an extended period.

In this example the employer had never explicitly said that particular 'sessional' workers were expected to attend work on a regular basis and to turn up for the shifts they were offered but there had been a subtle shift in the relationship over the four-year period and obligations had crept in where none had been at the beginning.

3.2.3 Distinguishing between employed and self-employed workers

Some organisations attempt to get round the problem of properly identifying who has which rights by accepting suggestions from their staff that they are self-employed or by offering posts on a freelance or self-employed basis.

This does not always work, and it can be expensive if it does not. A detailed discussion of the distinction between employed and self-employed workers is beyond the scope of this book but independent tests of the distinction have been evolved by the Inland Revenue, the DSS and the courts. The fact that a sessional worker is doing work for other organisations can be a relevant factor but it will not be the whole story if there are other features of the relationship which point to employment, such as the existence of a line manager and the requirement to comply with a code of conduct. A detailed discussion of the distinction is to be found in *The Voluntary Sector Legal Handbook* (see Resources).

3.2.4 Documentation

The documentation the organisation prepares for its different categories of staff is a vital part of the picture but again it cannot be the whole story. Even an agreement which says that a worker is not an employee and is not obliged to accept work when it is offered will be overruled by a court if the overall evidence points to a relationship of employer and employee.

Having said that, it is very important for the documentation not to undermine what the organisation is trying to achieve. Agreements with sessional, bank, agency or genuinely self-employed workers should not offer terms and conditions which are appropriate only to employees. Employers may need to take advice on the kinds of contract or agreement they should be issuing to their various employees.

3.3 What employers should do

A key job for managers is to monitor the categories of staff employed and to be aware of when the status of a particular worker may have changed. This means:

- keeping records of which shifts each sessional worker works, from when they start with the organisation, putting reporting procedures in place to deal with any concerns that arise over a worker's status;

- reviewing the position with a sessional worker if they appear to have taken up a pattern of regular work for the organisation;

- reviewing on a regular basis (say every six months) the position of workers whose status is unclear and making adjustments if appropriate, in consultation with the worker concerned;

- being aware of the equality issues which arise when part-timers are treated differently and offering pro rata benefits to part-time employees.

Are zero hours contracts the answer?

Some organisations offer zero hours contracts as the solution to the potentially expensive trap of a casual or sessional worker becoming unintentionally an employee. Zero hours contracts have been understandably criticised when used exploitatively by employers. But in organisations where work levels fluctuate unpredictably they can be a positive response. They acknowledge the employment status of the worker and offer a framework of rights, but avoid a guarantee by the employer of any particular amount of work.

An employee on a zero hours contract might be eligible for SSP if the statutory requirements were met. The employer might also be prepared to offer contractual sick pay on the basis of a certain number of days for a certain number of weeks worked over say a six or

---

twelve-month period. Holiday could be calculated in a similar way. In other respects the zero hours employee would have the full range of statutory rights to time off, maternity leave etc.. The management of these absences would if anything be easier for the employer, who could offer the work to another employee on a zero hours contract when a particular employee was unavailable.

Chapter Four

Statutory Rights to Time Off and Involvement in Court Proceedings

The law on time off from work is set out in the Employment Rights Act 1996 (ERA) and the Trade Union and Labour Relations Consolidation Act 1992 (TULR(C)A). There are also several codes of practice setting out guidelines for employers and employees. These are:

- the Code of Practice for Time Off for Trade Union Duties and Activities (ACAS);
- the Code of Practice on Safety Representatives and Safety Committees (HSC);
- the Code of Practice on Time Off for the Training of Safety Representatives (HSC).

There is a range of circumstances in which employees are entitled by statute to take time off from work, sometimes with pay and sometimes without. However, the rules do not give employees absolute rights regardless of the circumstances of the employer. Generally, tribunals which are asked to hear complaints about the refusal of time off where there is a statutory right will consider:

- the effect of the time off on the employer's business;
- the size of the organisation;
- the possibility of providing cover for absent employees.

Hence, a local authority would be expected to comply more readily with requests for time off than a small local voluntary organisation with only a handful of paid employees. Statutory time off is not unlimited. The law provides that:

- the amount of time off, and
- the occasions on which time off is taken, and
- any conditions to which the taking of time off is subject must be reasonable in all the circumstances.

Examples

In one case a part-time NALGO officer was refused ten days leave to produce a union magazine. The tribunal found that this was reasonable because he was already permitted 12 weeks leave per year to participate in the work of 22 union committees.

In another case involving public duties a tribunal rejected an employee's claim for 124 days off per year (over half his normal working time) where he wished to take on extra duties for a local council and a Planning Board. The tribunal considered his role in the employer's business and thought that it would not be reasonable to expect the employer to give him any more than 45 days off each year [*Phizacklea* v. *Vickers Shipbuilding Ltd* COIT 1523/52].

It is possible to dismiss someone for taking time off if they abuse a statutory right.

Example

A tribunal found that an infant school fairly dismissed a teacher who refused to ask his employer's consent before taking time off to engage in his duties as a local councillor. The teacher said that in his view he did not need to ask permission to take time off but merely to notify the headmistress that he would be taking it. The employer did not agree and nor did the tribunal [*Halfpenny* v. *Our Lady's Preparatory School* EAT 468/83].

Taking action against an employee can lead to automatic penalties in the tribunal, if the tribunal takes the view that the employer is penalising an employee for exercising a statutory right.

4.1 Trade union officials

Many employers, particularly those who are anxious to offer a fair deal (or better) to their staff, fall into the trap of thinking that the rights of trade union officials and trade union members are sacrosanct. They are not. However, trade union officials and members can generally be relied upon to know what their rights are.

The significance of these rights will be hugely increased if the government implements its 1997 proposals on compulsory recognition of unions. At present officials of independent trade unions recognised by their employers have the right with permission to take paid time off during working hours to carry out specified duties. 'Officials' includes shop stewards and branch officers (TULR(C)A S168).

The specified duties are defined in TULR(C)A S168. Broadly they are duties connected with collective bargaining which is defined in TULR(C)A S178(2) as including:

- terms and conditions;
- hiring, firing and suspension;
- allocation of work;
- discipline;
- trade union membership;
- machinery for negotiation with the employer.

The employer must have recognised the union and agreed to the duties concerned being carried out by it. Officials may also seek time off for approved training for the duties covered by the Act. The training must be approved by the official's own union or by the TUC.

4.1.1 The amount of time off

The amount and frequency of a trade union official's absences must be reasonable in the circumstances. There is detailed guidance in the ACAS Code of Practice (see Resources at the back of this book) which recommends a formal agreement between the employer and the union covering:

- the amount of time off permitted;
- when time off can be taken;
- when it will be paid;
- how it should be requested.

Example

In *Daniels* v. *GLC* (COIT 1061/201) when a shop steward requested two days off for training in discrimination law the employer refused because the official had recently attended a ten day course on the subject. The tribunal found this refusal was reasonable.

4.1.2 The right to pay

If the official obtains the employer's prior permission for time off, then they are entitled to paid time off (TULR(C)A S169(1)). If they do not obtain permission, they lose the right for it to be paid. The official should be paid normal wages for time off. Officials who work variable hours should have normal pay based on average earnings (TULR(C)A S169(4)) or, where this cannot be calculated, by reference to the pay of comparable colleagues.

4.1.3 Remedies for denial of time off

Employees should consider the availability of internal procedures before taking action in the tribunal. If there is an agreement with the employer on time off this may well contain a complaints or grievance procedure. If not, the normal grievance procedure could be used. However, a union official who has been denied time off in breach of the statute or has been denied pay can complain to the tribunal within three months of the employer's refusal. Tribunals rarely award compensation unless the employer has allowed time off but failed to pay the employee for it. However, if the tribunal finds that the employer has failed to grant time off when it should have done, it must make a declaration of what the employee's rights are so that the employer can comply in the future. It is automatically unfair to dismiss a trade union official where the only or principal reason for the dismissal was the official's assertion of the right to time off or to be paid for time off.

4.1.4 What employers should do

Written agreements are obviously useful in large organisations with complex hierarchies and recognised unions. In smaller organisations the management time involved in negotiating an agreement on time off will have to be balanced against the time likely to be spent handling requests on a case by case basis. In most cases it will be better to lay out the ground rules beforehand to avoid disputes.

Compulsory recognition of unions, if and when introduced by the government, will make the management of time off for union duties a significant issue once more. Increasing numbers of employers have avoided it in recent years by de-recognition.

4.2 Those participating in trade union activities

There is a right under S170 of TULR(C)A to take time off during working hours without pay to participate in trade union activities. As with the right to paid time off for union officials this right will become very much more important if there is legislation on compulsory recognition.

4.2.1 Who may claim

The right is available to members of independent trade unions recognised by the employer. An employee claiming the right must fall into the category of worker for which the union is recognised.

4.2.2 The activities covered

The right covers:

- any activities of the union;
- any activities in relation to which the employee is acting as a representative of the union.

To qualify as a union activity an activity must have a 'genuine link' to the relationship between the union, staff and employer. Ultimately, it is a question of fact whether an activity can count as a union activity.

The ACAS Code offers the following examples:

- attending normal meetings;
- voting in elections and ballots;
- participating in union committees and conferences.

In *Wignall v. British Gas Corporation* (1984 IRLR 493) the right to ten days unpaid leave to participate in producing a union magazine was found by the tribunal to be covered.

4.2.3 The amount of time off

Again it must be 'reasonable in all the circumstances' and employers should follow the ACAS guidelines. The needs of the employer must be balanced against the right. It is therefore reasonable for an employer to look at how much time an employee has already had off for trade union duties and activities, in deciding whether to grant a particular request.

4.2.4 Remedies for denial of time off

An employee who has been denied time off to pursue union activities can complain to the tribunal within three months of the denial. The tribunal may make a declaration and can award compensation though it rarely does so. Dismissing an employee where the reason or principal reason was the assertion of the statutory right is automatically unfair.

4.2.5 The right to pay

There is no statutory right to pay for time taken off to engage in union activities. However, employers and unions may negotiate an agreement which allows for pay in specified circumstances. The ACAS Code recommends an agreement on time off for union duties and activities and the Code suggests that allowing for pay for specified union activities can help to ensure that, for example, workplace meetings are fully representative.

4.3 Workplace safety representatives – unionised workforces

Properly appointed safety representatives have the right to paid time off during working hours to carry out their statutory duties. Only safety representatives appointed by recognised trade unions with collective bargaining negotiating rights are covered. The union must notify the employer of the names of the elected representatives and the group of employees they are to cover. Regulations state that elected safety representatives should if possible have at least two years service with the employer or at least two years experience of similar work. This is not an absolute requirement.

The duty of safety representatives is to monitor and investigate safety standards in the workplace and to make representations to the employer where appropriate.

4.3.1 The amount of time off

The amount of time off is that which is necessary for the safety representative to carry out statutory duties properly and to undergo reasonable training. The Code of Practice issued by the Health and Safety Commission on the training, role and functions of safety representatives provides guidance. The Code recommends that all new safety representatives receive basic training in health and safety issues after their appointment, followed by training specific to their workplace. The training facilities should be approved by the union or by the TUC. Employers should be given a few weeks notice of the course and should be shown the syllabus if they request it.

4.3.2 The rate of pay

Safety representatives should be paid their normal rate during time off carrying out their duties. If there is no normal rate of pay then average hourly earnings for that or a comparable job should be used as the basis (as for trade union officials).

4.3.3 Remedies for denial of time off

Safety representatives denied time off or pay during time off can complain to the industrial tribunal, which can make a declaration or award compensation. They also have the right not to be subjected to a detriment or to be dismissed for carrying out or proposing to carry out their functions (ERA S44). These rights carry no minimum qualifying period or upper age limit (normally the right to allege unfair dismissal is lost at the age of 65) and dismissal in these circumstance will be automatically unfair (ERA S100).

4.4 Employee safety representatives in workplaces with no recognised union

Since 1st October 1996 employers in workplaces with no recognised unions have been under an obligation to consult with their staff on matters concerning their health and safety at work (Health and

Safety (Consultation with Employees) Regulations 1996 (SI 1996 No 1513)). This consultation can be carried out directly with the workforce or, if employees prefer, with elected safety representatives.

The functions of elected safety representatives are:

- to make representations to the employer about workplace hazards;
- to make general representations to the employer about health and safety;
- to represent employees in workplace consultation with inspectors appointed under the Health and Safety at Work Act.

They should be offered reasonable training, and travel and subsistence costs while undertaking it.

4.4.1 The amount of time off

Employee safety representatives should be given as much time off with pay as is necessary for them to carry out their functions, to undergo reasonable amounts of training and stand as candidates in the election of representatives. As with safety representatives in unionised workplaces the test is what is necessary rather than what is reasonable.

4.4.2 The amount of pay

The amount of pay is calculated in the same way as the pay of safety representatives in unionised workforces.

4.4.3 Remedies for denial of time off

Employee safety representatives or candidates in elections can apply to the industrial tribunal if they are denied time off or pay for time off. The tribunal can award compensation or make a declaration. They also have the right not to be subjected to any detriment or to be dismissed for standing as candidates in safety elections or carrying out their functions as safety representatives. These rights carry no minimum qualifying period or upper age limit.

4.5 Time off for public duties

Certain public duties specified in S50 of the ERA carry the right to reasonable amounts of time off without pay. The duties which count are changed from time to time. At present the right is available to justices of the peace and to members of:

- a local authority;
- a statutory tribunal;
- police authority;
- a board of prison visitors or prison visiting committee;
- a relevant health body e.g. a community health council;
- a relevant education body e.g. the governing body of a school;
- the Environment Agency or the Scottish Environment Protection Agency.

The duties which carry the right to time off are attendance at meetings of the body concerned and doing anything that is approved by the body concerned in order to carry out its functions.

For jury service see Section 4.9.

4.5.1 The amount of time off

A reasonableness test is applied. An employee cannot have unlimited time off or time off whenever they are called upon to attend a meeting or perform a duty. How much time off, when it is taken, and any conditions which apply to it, should be reasonable in all the circumstances taking into account:

- how much time off is needed for that particular public office in general and for this particular duty;
- how much time off the employee may already have had for other statutory reasons such as trade union duties;
- the general circumstances of the employer's business and the effect of the proposed absence on that business.

4.5.2 The right to pay

There is no statutory right to payment, although in practice many employers are prepared to pay employees who are engaged in public duties.

However, local authorities are limited by S10 of the Local Government and Housing Act 1989 in the amount they are permitted to pay to staff engaged in public duties.

4.5.3 Remedies for denial of time off

Employees have three months to present a claim to the tribunal if they are denied time off to perform public duties. Tribunals can make a declaration or award compensation if they uphold a complaint. They have no power to impose conditions or stipulate, for example, how much time off should be allowed.

4.5.4 What employers should do

Employers need to know from the earliest possible time whether a particular member of staff has a need for time off to carry out public duties. It is a question which can legitimately be put on job application forms or at interview.

If an employee does need time off, the ground rules need to be established straight away. This might be at the very start of employment, or when an employee acquires public office during the course of employment.

How much time should be allowed off for public duties?

There is no code of practice as there is for union duties and activities. However, the following factors will be important in striking a balance between the needs of the employer's business and the requirements of the employee's public duties:

- whether there were any relevant discussions at the employee's interview;
- whether the contract of employment contains any relevant provisions;
- whether the employer already has a procedure for dealing with requests for time off (if there is a procedure it should be followed unless there are factors which would justify departing from it);
- whether the employee has already been given time off for other purposes and if so how much;
- the nature of the employee's job and how critical the employee's presence is to the business;
- how easy it is to provide cover;
- the size of the employee's workload;
- whether there are any conditions which the employer wishes to impose. (Reasonable conditions can be imposed as long as these do not make it impractical for the employee to take time off or impose a penalty such as depriving the employee of the chance to work overtime.)

Tribunal decisions show that both employers and employees are expected to be flexible. Employers might be expected to use the employee's wages during time off to provide cover. Employees, on the other hand, might be expected to give up some of their holiday for some of their public duties.

Examples

Size of the employer

In a case involving Lloyds Bank the tribunal placed emphasis on the size of the employer and the fact that the employee concerned did not have a special role. The tribunal thought it was reasonable to expect the bank to provide cover from its very large workforce [*Bone* v. *Lloyds Bank Ltd* COIT 914/75].

Availability of cover

In another case a teacher was refused a request for time off to perform some of his duties as a local councillor. At the time, industrial action by the teaching unions had led to a shortage of supply teachers. The tribunal found that in these particular circumstances the employer's refusal was reasonable [*Evans* v. *Mid Glamorgan County Council* COIT 1720/123].

In another case a worker was responsible for dealing with export customers and his job required personal knowledge of his clients. Before promotion to this position he had been allowed 26 days off a year to sit as a JP. After promotion he asked for further time to sit on the juvenile panel. The tribunal said the employer's refusal was reasonable because the element of personal contact in the job meant that it was not easily covered by other staff [*Gardner* v. *F H Lloyd & Co Ltd* COIT 900/38].

The effect on the employer's business will often be the decisive factor in a tribunal case.

For example, a qualified shift supervisor whose presence was essential for the production process to take place at all was refused seven days leave per year to perform his duties as a magistrate. His employer's business was in severe financial difficulty at the time and the tribunal said that he should be permitted a maximum of five days, taking the rest from his own free time [*Ward* v. *Bridon Steel Ltd* COIT 1256/43].

4.6 Employee representatives in non-unionised workforces – redundancies and transfers of undertakings

Reasonable paid time off is available to employee representatives elected to consult on collective redundancies (now defined as redundancies involving more than 20 employees over a three-month period) or a transfer of an undertaking (ERA S61).

There are no guidelines in the statute as to how elections should be carried out. This has to be worked out by the employer and the employees. However, candidates in any workplace election have the same rights as elected representatives.

4.6.1 The amount of time off and pay

The amount of time off and the amount of pay are worked out according to the same criteria and principles as apply to the carrying out of union duties. However there is no Code of Practice.

4.6.2 Remedies for denial of time off

Refusal of time off or refusal to pay entitles the employee to bring a complaint to the tribunal. Employee representatives also have a right not to suffer a detriment as a consequence of having performed or proposing to perform their duties (ERA S47). Dismissal of an employee on the grounds that he or she has carried out or proposes to carry out activities as an employee representative will be deemed automatically unfair (ERA S103). The normal minimum qualifying period and upper age limit for unfair dismissal claims do not apply.

Complaints concerning refusal of time off, refusal of payment, subjection to a detriment or dismissal must be taken to the tribunal within three months of the complaint arising.

4.7 Pension scheme trustees

Employees who are trustees of occupational pension schemes are entitled by S58 of the ERA to paid time off to carry out the duties of a trustee, or to undergo training relevant to those duties.

4.7.1 The amount of time off

The amount of time off is that which would be reasonable in all the circumstances, taking into account the effect of the employee's absence on the employer's business.

4.7.2 The amount of pay

Where the employee has normal working hours, the amount of pay should be normal pay. Where the hours are variable, pay should be calculated by reference to average hourly earnings (as for those carrying out union duties).

4.7.3 Remedies for denial of time off

Employees who are pension scheme trustees have:

- the right to reasonable time off;
- the right to pay during time off;
- the right not to subjected to any detriment for performing the duties of trusteeship;
- the right not to be dismissed for performing the duties of trusteeship.

They may complain to the tribunal if any of these rights are infringed. Tribunals may award just and equitable compensation as well as making appropriate declarations.

A dismissal on the grounds of pension scheme trusteeship is automatically unfair regardless of length of service. There is also no upper age limit for bringing such a claim.

4.8 Redundancy

An employee who is under notice of dismissal by reason of redundancy has a right to reasonable paid time off during working hours to look for a new job, or to undertake or arrange training for future work (S52 of the ERA 1996).

4.8.1 The right to time off

Only employees who have been given notice of redundancy to take place on a particular date are eligible for paid time off. The right does not arise when the employer has simply made it known that redundancies are likely. The right is also only available to those with two years continuous service at the date the notice period expires (or any statutory notice period to which the employee is entitled, if longer).

The right is not lost even if the right to a redundancy payment has been lost, e.g. by a refusal of a reasonable offer of suitable alternative employment.

4.8.2 The amount of time off

The amount of time off is that which is reasonable, taking into account the needs of the employee and those of the employer's business.

4.8.3 The rate of pay

The time off should be paid at the normal hourly rate subject to a maximum for the entire redundancy notice period of 40 per cent of one week's pay. In practice many employers offer more pay than this, either through a commitment in the contract of employment or through collective bargaining. If there is no normal hourly rate the amount is calculated by reference to average working hours and pay over a 12-week period. A week is deemed to end on a Saturday unless the employee is paid weekly, in which case it ends on the day that payment is made (ERA S235(1)).

4.8.4 Remedies for denial of time off

An employee who is denied time off, or payment for time off, can complain to the tribunal within three months. The tribunal can make a declaration as to how much time should have been allowed, or compensate the employee with pay up to the statutory amount of 40 per cent of one week's pay.

4.8.5 What employers should do

Employees who are under notice of redundancy are likely to be lacking in motivation, and inclined to maximise opportunities to be absent from work. This is a fact of life; the employer who has told an employee that his or her services are no longer required has to make a balanced decision about the extent to which it will scrutinise the redundant employee's reasons for absence. If the employee's presence during the redundancy notice period is critical, the employer must make it very clear that time off will only be paid if the employee can provide reasonable evidence that they were looking for work or arranging training.

Type of right	Amount of time off	Right to pay or not?	How much pay?	Who is eligible?	Remedies
Trade union officials	Reasonable (ACAS Code)	Yes	Normal	Shop stewards branch officers; officials of recognised unions	
Trade union members	Reasonable (ACAS Code)	No	By negotiation/contract	Members of recognised union	IT within three months for compensation and/or declaration. Automatic unfair dismissal and protection from detriment short of dismissal
Safety reps (union)	As necessary for duties and training (HSC Code)	Yes	Normal	Reps appointed by recognised union with collective bargaining negotiating rights	
Safety reps (no union); candidates for election	As necessary for duties, training and election	Yes	Normal	Reps elected by workforce where no recognised union	
Public duties	Reasonable	No	By negotiation/contract	JPs, members of local authority, statutory tribunal, police authority, board of prison visitors, health body, education body, Environment Agency	IT within three months for compensation and/or declaration
Employee reps; redundancies and TUPE	Reasonable	Yes	Normal	Reps elected by workforce where no recognised union	IT within three months for compensation and/or declaration. Automatic unfair dismissal protection and protection from detriment short of dismissal
Pension scheme trustees	Reasonable	Yes	Normal	Trustees of occupational pension schemes	"
Redundancy	Reasonable	Yes	2–5 weeks pay during redundancy notice period	Employees under notice of redundancy	IT within three months for compensation and/or declaration

4.8.6 **Table of statutory rights**

4.9 Jury service

A requirement to attend court takes precedence over all other obligations which might affect an employee, including the obligations set out in the contract of employment. The contract might confirm the employers intention to comply when an employee could be required to attend court. Any attempt by an employer, through the contract or otherwise, to impede an employee who is required to go to court, for whatever reason, is likely to amount to contempt of court. This is itself an offence which can result in fines or imprisonment or both. In practice, courts do treat very seriously any action towards employees which could amount to a contempt on the employers part.

Anyone between the ages of 18 and 70 can be called for jury service unless they are exempt. Those exempt include people involved in the administration of justice such as lawyers and court staff, the clergy, those with serious criminal convictions and people with mental disorders.

A person might be excused jury service if they can show good reason for being unable to attend. The needs of an employer could constitute a good reason, as could the fact that the person called to do service is the sole or main carer of young children. An employee who is neither exempt nor excused must attend for jury service, and must be permitted to do so by the employer. It is a serious contempt of court to dismiss or threaten to dismiss an employee who has been called for jury service.

There is no entitlement to pay from the employer, although many employers do continue to pay staff during jury service. Employees can claim some compensation from the court.

4.9.1 Long trials

Potential jurors whose work situation would be jeopardised by participation in a long trial should make this clear to the Jury Summoning Officer at the time they are called for jury service. Letters in support from employers may help but the court will not accept direct requests from employers without consulting the employee first. Courts will try to comply with requests to be excused from long trials if they have sufficient jurors available who are able to participate without difficulty.

4.9.2 What employers should do

Jury service is a fact of life and something which in most circumstances an employer will be expected to accommodate. However, if it would be harmful to the organisation or business to release a person for jury service at a particular time, the employee can apply to the Jury Summoning Officer to have the jury service deferred or postponed indefinitely. A letter or other evidence from the employer will obviously help, although courts will never accept requests for postponement from an employer without checking with the employee first.

There is a right of appeal to the judge in the particular case against a refusal to defer or postpone. Enquiries about jury service should be addressed to the Jury Bailiff Section of the court which sent out the jury summons. Generally the court will try to accommodate requests for postponement or deferral from essential workers, or others with sound work related reasons, but the decision will depend on the availability of jurors at the time of the request.

The contract of employment should say whether staff on jury service are entitled to be paid. If they are, the contract should also require them to hand over to the employer any payments of compensation received from the court. Rates of compensation are set out from time to time in Home Office Circulars. As of March 1998 the maximum rates were £22.40 for a day of four hours or less and £44.80 for over four hours, rising to £89.60 for each day after the tenth day of service. There are also subsistence and travelling allowances.

4.10 Attendance at court

Anybody, whether employed or not, can become involved as a party in court proceedings or be asked to appear as a witness in civil or criminal proceedings in a court or tribunal. Employers have no choice about releasing employees who are themselves parties to a court case. However, unless there is a clause in the contract of employment giving the right to attend court as a witness, the employer is under no obligation to release an employee for this purpose.

Generally, however, it is good practice to do so. If an employee's participation in the court proceedings is vital, a witness order of some description is likely to ensue if the employer refuses to release the employee concerned. The employer would be in contempt of court if they did not permit the employee to comply with a witness order. This would also place the employee in contempt.

There is no obligation to pay an employee who is absent in order to attend court as a party or a witness, unless the contract of employment says that such absences will be paid. Otherwise it is a matter for discussion between employer and employee.

4.11 Imprisonment

An employee may have to be absent from work in order to serve a prison sentence or during a period on remand. It will often be the case that a term of imprisonment has the effect of ending the employment contract, but this is not the only possible outcome.

The fact that an employee has been given a prison sentence does not give the employer an automatic right to terminate the employment. This would risk a claim of unfair or wrongful dismissal. Employers must act fairly and reasonably in dealing with imprisoned members of staff. A prisoner on remand, for example, might not be found guilty. An employer who dismissed, them without waiting for the decision of the criminal court could be found to have unfairly dismissed. Alternatively, if the offence in question has nothing to do with the work the employee is employed to do and the sentence is relatively short, a tribunal might decide that a reasonable employer would have found a replacement for the duration of the sentence.

4.11.1 Payment during imprisonment

There is no need to continue to pay an employee who is unable to work because of imprisonment. It is clear that unless there is a statutory or contractual right to payment, a person who does not attend work is not entitled to be paid.

4.11.2 'Frustration' of the contract

Sometimes the length of the term in prison means that the employment contract is effectively 'frustrated'. A frustrated contract is one which cannot be carried out because circumstances prevent it. If frustration occurs, neither party needs to give notice to the other and there is no dismissal; hence there can be no claim for wrongful or unfair dismissal by the employee.

However, it is difficult for an employer to judge whether a court would find that a prison sentence had frustrated a contract. A better course of action is to conduct a fair procedure allowing the employee to put their side of the story, and dismissing the employee on notice if this seems appropriate. If the employee is in prison at the time the decision has to be made, then the employer will have to communicate through the employee's solicitor.

4.11.3 What employers should do

When a member of staff is imprisoned, the employer is expected to act reasonably in all the circumstances. They should neither dismiss as a knee jerk response nor make special effort to accommodate the imprisoned employee where it would place great strain on the organisation to do so. Before deciding whether to dismiss an imprisoned member of staff consider the following factors:

- the length of the imprisonment. There are no hard and fast rules, but a short prison term – say three months – is more likely to mean that the employer should hold the post open than a longer term of, say, a year or more;
- the employee's standards of work and disciplinary record;
- the employee's length of service;
- the importance of that particular employee to the organisation and how easily they could be replaced on a temporary basis;
- whether the imprisonment is on remand or follows a conviction;
- whether the offence affects the employee's ability to do the job. It would be reasonable for an organisation providing services to children to dismiss an employee convicted of a sexual assault on a child. It might not be reasonable to dismiss an employee imprisoned for a drink driving offence if driving forms no part of the employee's duties.

Examples

A company director was imprisoned for almost two years. He delegated the running of the company to someone else during this time, but some meetings were held in the prison. He also established an arrangement enabling him to be absent from directors' meetings during the prison term. The company became insolvent and the director applied to the Secretary of State for a redundancy payment. The Secretary of State argued that he had not been employed whilst he was in prison. The tribunal rejected this view and held that his contract had not been terminated, either by dismissal or frustration during the prison term [*Moore* v. *Secretary of State for Employment* COIT 1512/196].

In another case, an employee who was sentenced to a short term of imprisonment for fine default applied for the term to be deferred and arranged with the employer to take it as annual leave. When he was later dismissed, the tribunal confirmed that his continuity of employment had not been affected by his imprisonment and that he therefore had the right to protection from unfair dismissal [*Maltby* v. *Bil-Co Soft Drinks* COIT 1447/191].

95233

Chapter Five

Sickness

5.1 General

5.1.1 Balancing the needs of the organisation and employee

All organisations have staff absences due to illness or other personal reasons such as bereavement. A certain level of sickness is normal; a higher than average level may be acceptable; but for every organisation there is going to be a level that is not considered acceptable. Where a particular employee cannot carry out their work due to sickness, the organisation has to make a carefully balanced set of decisions. That balance is between the employee's need for time to recover to full health and the organisation's need to provide services efficiently and to maintain staff morale. The balance can be achieved as even-handedly as possible only within a negotiated policy on managing sickness absence. Many voluntary organisations are now developing these.

A policy provides boundaries for employees and employers to work within. Managers can then deal with all cases of sickness absence with sensitivity and understanding, treating each case in a fair, consistent and constructive manner. With a detailed policy, management action can relate to standards and precedents rather than having to start from scratch for each case. This latter route often leads to claims of favouritism or unfairness and to resentment among other staff. Worse, it may lead to complaints of discrimination on grounds of race, sex or disability.

An individual case may occasionally push those boundaries and require some flexibility. You must always be able to justify a particular action on clear organisational or compassionate grounds, not personal ones, even if the policy failed to cover that specific case.

A policy for managing sickness absence is not a disciplinary policy by another name. Action dealing with absence may eventually lead to dismissal, but staff need to be reassured that the motivation is primarily to ensure a healthy workforce. The policy ensures that consistent management action occurs soon after the sickness absence occurs. It is only appropriate for matters related to sickness absence to be dealt with under the organisation's disciplinary procedure initially, where a line manager suspects that a worker has not been honest about their absence.

5.1.2 Issues affecting organisational ability to deal with sickness absence

Organisational culture. The culture of the organisation and its current attitude to dealing with absence due to sickness. Where it is only acceptable to be off sick if you are hospitalised, people who feel really ill but do not look ill may never feel justified in taking time off. This leads to stress and poor morale. These cultural issues have a profound and often relatively hidden impact on how sickness absence is handled and may need to be made explicit before they can be tackled. There is more on this in Chapter 1.

Management structure and management line responsibility. The management structure and attitudes to management will affect how well the policy works. If managers are not used to exercising line authority they will find it hard to act according to the guidelines. The structure needs to be in place to ensure consistency of application across the organisation.

Junior or new managers may need support in being authoritative in this area. They may mistake *authoritative* action for *authoritarian* action and need coaching in how to apply the guidelines fairly to staff without compromising organisational needs.

Lack of control over one's own work has been shown to be the highest cause of stress among white collar workers. This could be a consequence of poor job design or a manager who has no skills in delegation and retains control over all functions to the detriment of staff. Managers' own behaviour can result in absence if they adopt a style which is felt as bullying or intimidatory. Other common causes of stress in the workplace are:

- unclear or ambiguous job descriptions;
- unrealistic deadlines;
- inability to accomplish objectives;
- misunderstanding the reward system;
- unclear supervisory responsibilities;
- unsatisfactory pay, benefits or job security;
- unhealthy work climate;
- excessive competition as opposed to collaboration;
- conflicts between groups;
- overemphasised task as opposed to people management philosophies;
- conflicting personal and organisational goals;
- unfulfilled career goals;
- lack of opportunity for growth and development;
- under-utilisation or over-utilisation of abilities.

(Quoted by Moira Halliday in 'Stress Audit Report' February 1997, unpublished.)

Managing change. Introducing any new policies or procedures involves **managing change**. This has an impact on how people work and communicate and also on perceptions about how management is treating staff. Existing staff must understand the reasons for change and have an opportunity to comment on proposals. This is not only good practice but is also good for morale, and for motivation to co-operate and to work well for the organisation. Changes in reporting or management actions need to be monitored up the line to make sure all managers understand the same by the policy. Existing staff need updating and new staff need information as part of their induction.

Act within the law. All organisations have to act within the law. The law has a huge amount to say about:

- management procedures in relation to potential unfair dismissal claims;
- varying the contract when you introduce new systems;
- health and safety;
- access to medical records;
- sickness reporting and SSP;
- not acting in a discriminatory way;
- statutory rights to time off.

This means that any procedures have to be introduced and managed with care. Should your organisation ever be taken to an Employment Tribunal, your processes may end up under external legal scrutiny! (See Section 1.3.3 and Chapters 2, 3, 4 and 5.)

5.1.3 Pre-employment health checks

A pre-employment health check is where some or all new employees are required to provide information about their current state of health and recent health history. The arguments in favour of this are that it can provide an employer with information concerning the likely capability of the employee and whether their potential absence rate will be higher than the average. It can also help the employer to organise the job to reduce any health difficulties – for example, reducing time spent in areas of high pollution by a person with asthma. This is a fairly common practice in some sectors, but has its limitations as a tool and has implications under the Disability Discrimination Act. Although no organisation wants to take on staff who cannot carry out their work because of ill-health, checking whether they are healthy and capable when they arrive has its problems.

Limiting absence – what are you checking for? Some organisations may use the practice as, effectively, 'gatekeeping' or turning away candidates whose physical or psychological fitness is in question. This has worrying implications for the individual's lifetime of employment. Is a person's health going to be in question for ever more if they have a period of ill-health which may never recur? Are we to assume that only the fittest individuals can work most effectively? And how is 'health' determined?

Example of the effect of health screening

A psychiatric occupational therapist had three weeks off for 'stress'. She had been finding the job increasingly difficult to manage and she had recently left her partner. Her GP signed her off for three weeks, with no medication. A few months later she successfully applied for a job as an occupational therapist for work in a different area. She had to fill in a medical form. The occupational health department queried her absence for stress and contacted her GP. As this process took several weeks, it was very worrying. The new job, which seemed to be very suitable, was jeopardised. Fortunately, in this case the applicant was eventually accepted.

The assumptions behind assessing an individual's suitability for a post, must be examined extremely carefully.

There is evidence to show that manual workers, workers from areas of the country with higher poverty rates and women workers have higher absence rates than other groups. If taken to its logical extreme, pre-employment health screening could result in some groups, who are already disadvantaged in terms of health, being labelled as less capable for work.

Pre-employment health checks will not stop employees taking time off because the children are sick. Nor will they deal with absence due to boredom, hangovers or poor motivation.

Some health checks may be necessary for insurance purposes (see Chapter 10). There are also circumstances in which pre-employment health screening may be justified on health and safety grounds. For example an employee with an infectious disease could endanger the lives of clients with immune deficiency or other conditions.

Relationship to the Disability Discrimination Act. Most organisations using health screening will ask prospective employees to fill in a health questionnaire. Before confirming the offer of the post, they then only send for screening those whose questionnaires give cause for concern. It has been the practice of some firms to take people on even if their check shows that they might become more ill in the near future, but not to allow them to join the occupational health insurance scheme. This may be illegal under the DDA, if the employer is covered by the Act.

The DDA makes it illegal to discriminate against people with disabilities both in the selection procedure and in the terms under which they are employed, although not in relation to occupational pension schemes. It also requires employers to make reasonable adjustments to the workplace to enable people with differing levels of ability to work effectively. There have been no cases regarding pre-employment screening as yet. However, this could be a prime area of concern (see Chapter 7 on Disability and Absence and Chapter 10 on Making Financial Provision).

Conclusion. It is important for organisations to employ staff who are competent, particularly in small voluntary organisations where one individual with a high level of absence can cause a serious difficulty in service delivery. Pre-employment health screening is a legitimate way of looking at the potential capability of a new worker. However, it must be carried out very carefully.

Screening has an inevitable limitation; it can only provide a snapshot of the individual at that moment, it cannot be a reliable predictor of future sickness absence. Any pre-employment health screening must be applied to all employees, and must test the ability of the employee to carry out the work that they are required to do.

Health checks should always be carried out by a qualified person in occupational health who has knowledge of the job in question and the likely limiting factors of the post and how they might match to the individual's health record in question. If the health record does show high levels of absence in the past this should be investigated carefully, not automatically used as a reason for ruling out a person from that post.

No person must be discriminated against on the grounds of disability alone, whether or not the employer is covered by the Act. An employer covered by the DDA, should provide reasonable adjustments to enable the employee to work for them and will be liable under the Act if they fail to do so. They will have to justify why they should not make the adjustments necessary for the individual.

5.2 Health promotion and health and safety

5.2.1 Good for staff, good for organisation

Healthy organisations not only employ competent staff but also care about the work environment and resources staff have to work with. They take their responsibilities seriously under the Health and Safety at Work legislation and provide adequate time and resources for risk assessments to be carried out and acted on.

The management of the health and welfare of workers:

- helps performance;
- lowers absenteeism;
- improves morale;
- reduces risk of injuries;
- reduces potential litigation claims in this area.

Even if you manage a small voluntary organisation, you are not exempt from these issues. You may even need to take extra care to ensure the premises and conditions are adequate because some funders have the attitude that service delivery is more important than the welfare of the staff delivering it. They won't fund what they see as a luxurious office space!

There are three main areas for management action:

- being pro-active about health and safety legislation implementation and risk assessments;
- encouraging staff to be trained in health and safety and in providing a safe environment;
- being pro-active on health promotion.

5.2.2 Legal minimum standards

The law requires employers to provide a safe and healthy working environment. Common law, Acts of Parliament and the European Union impose health and safety obligations on all employers in all workplaces. 'Workplaces' means any place that employees are required to work: this can be out of doors; in the employee's home; in the clients' home; in public. Although employers do not have control over these environments, they have an obligation to assess risks and ensure safe systems and procedures are in place. Where staff may be exposed to violence from clients or in public, these risks must be assessed and minimised. This may be done, for example, by: use of mobile phones; personal alarms; visits in pairs to certain areas; checking in and out systems. Chapter 2 Section 1, covers the legal standards in more detail.

In addition it is important to note that pregnant and breastfeeding workers have the right to rest facilities, conveniently near to washrooms and toilets, and if necessary the facility to lie down.

5.2.3 Safe environment – examples of conditions

There are many areas covered in the legislation concerning the office environment. A risk assessment must be carried out for all risks in all workplaces. There will be different rules in some voluntary organisations, for example, residential services, or arts organisations, such as theatres. The Health and Safety Executive will provide a comprehensive checklist of regulations applied to the physical work environment. The following are just some of the main areas and main requirements:

Some health and safety parameters

Space: Sufficient floor area, height and unoccupied space must be provided in any office. This means 11 cubic metres per person. The space taken up by the workstation is included, but space for filing cabinets and other equipment is excluded. Room height above three metres is not included in calculations.

Floors and surfaces: Floors must be soundly constructed and able to cope safely with loads placed on them. Surfaces must be free from holes, slopes or uneven patches.

Workstation: (the place where you work) must be appropriate for the individual and for the work, with equipment and materials within easy reach.

VDUs: Special regulations apply to people who use a VDU for a significant amount of their normal work. These are called the Display Screen Equipment Regulations 1992.

Light: There are specific and detailed regulations covering lights and the siting of lights especially in relation to computer screens.

Temperature: 16°C is the minimum acceptable temperature for primarily sedentary work. An upper limit is not specified, but 24°C is recommended by the World Health Organisation.

Smoking: A decision by the Employment Appeals Tribunal in October 1997 reinforced the right of employees to work in a smoke-free environment. The right to clean air weighs above the right to smoke. Employees must be provided with clean air and satisfactory ventilation.

Stress: This is becoming recognised as a major occupational health problem causing the estimated loss of 90 million working days per annum (Industrial Society). A recent TUC survey concluded that the voluntary sector was more stressful to work in than health, education or local government. Employers have an obligation under the law to ensure the health, safety and welfare at work of all employees. This means that where risks have been identified to an individual's health, action should be taken to prevent or reduce those risks. If this is not done and the individual employee can show that agreed action was not taken and their health suffered directly as a result, then the employer could find themselves liable to being sued (see Section 5.3.2 in this chapter).

Any employer should consider factors that are known to cause stress and be prepared to take action to minimise the risks associated with each one. These include:

- bullying;
- harassment;
- autocratic or erratic management;
- poor communication;
- overwork;
- lack of influences over work processes;
- working directly with the public.

Violence: In 1996 violence at work caused two deaths, 700 major injuries and 3,700 injuries leading to over three days absence due to violence at work according to the HSE statistics. Nursing staff and social care workers are the most likely to experience violence in the workplace. The HSE define violence as 'any incident in which the employee is abused, threatened or assaulted by a member of the public in circumstances arising out of their employment.' If violence from the public is a threat to staff, then a risk assessment must be carried out specifically on those risks. Staff who risk having to face violent situations should be trained in avoiding violence or de-escalating situations.

Suspension from work. Health and Safety Regulations give employees that right to be suspended on full pay in certain circumstances. These are as follows:

- When work could result in employees being exposed to a hazardous substance. In this case they are entitled to up to 26 weeks Medical Suspension Pay (MSP) at the normal rate (S64 ERA). There is a qualifying period of one month and the right is lost if the employee unreasonably refuses an offer of suitable alternative employment (which may be an offer of work which falls outside the employee's normal duties). The regulations are listed in S64(3) of the ERA.
- Dismissing an employee in order to avoid paying MSP gives grounds for a claim of unfair dismissal.

- When a woman is a new or expectant mother and the work is of a kind which could involve risk, by reason of her condition, to her health and safety or that of the child (Regulation 13A of the Management of Health and Safety at Work (Amendment) Regulations 1994). The risk must arise from processes or working conditions or physical, biological or chemical agents. There must be no reasonable way of avoiding the risk by altering hours of work or working conditions. There are also provisions covering night work.

- Suspension must be on normal pay and for a period as long as is necessary to avoid the risk. A woman denied pay has the right to complain to a tribunal.

It is automatically unfair to dismiss a new or expectant mother who is prohibited from working for health and safety reasons. The employer must either find suitable alternative employment or suspend the woman until the risk subsides.

5.2.4 Trained staff

The law provides that all employers should appoint 'competent' persons to carry out risk assessments. This should be seen as a management task, not the health and safety representative's task. 'Competent persons' should have:

- an understanding of the requirements of the law and best practice;
- an awareness of their own limitations;
- an understanding of the work activities being assessed;
- knowledge of the principles of risk assessment and prevention of hazards.

5.2.5 Specific health promotion

Despite the benefits of taking action on health awareness and health promotion, little action is taken by employers of any size, a survey by the Workplace Health Advisory Team (part of the HSE) shows. The health-related activities they most commonly had were:

- 72 per cent have a no-smoking policy (but 20 per cent had no plans to introduce one).
- 54 per cent provide health education materials.
- 40 per cent offer health screening to staff.

Example

East Midlands Electricity has taken action and claims that it has significantly reduced the number of days lost through sickness absence by introducing a scheme to manage back pain. Two years from the start of the programme it says that 94 per cent of staff who attended the course are still at work and 88 per cent in their normal job. The firm discovered that the average length of absence for back pain was eight months. After stress, backpain is the most commonly reported factor affecting work according to a 1993 EU study.

Some organisations offer:

- time off for cancer screening (NJC term in the *Green Book*);
- time off to attend health screening sessions or well person sessions;
- reduced or free membership of a leisure or health centre, health club or gym;
- showers so that staff can easily cycle or run to work, or exercise in the lunch hour.

5.3 Legal framework

The main legal concerns for a manager dealing with sickness absence are:

- to operate procedures fairly, consistently and, in particular, in a way which is not discriminatory under equal opportunities legislation;
- to ensure that if an employee is dismissed there is a genuine reason for it and the procedures used by the employer are fair.

Dismissal for sickness absence is potentially a fair reason for dismissal under s98 of the ERA, whether the sickness is short term and persistent or long term. However, the employer has a duty to act reasonably in any dismissal. This means that it must be reasonable to treat the employee's absence as a reason to dismiss and that the employer must follow fair procedures.

Employers have some flexibility in the way that they categorise sickness absence. However, cases usually fall into one of these categories:

- persistent short term absence, often for unconnected reasons;
- long term or chronic absence (which may arise from a disability);
- mental health/stress;
- malingering;
- pregnancy related illness.

There are different rules for each category.

5.3.1 Persistent short term absence

This is often characterised by lots of apparently unconnected minor illnesses. If the illnesses are not medically connected and if the employer reaches the point where dismissal is the only option, the potentially fair reason the employer will be relying on is 'some other substantial reason justifying dismissal'. The issue is not capability because it cannot really be said that someone who is off with flu one week, headache the next, and a stomach bug two weeks later, has a condition which makes them incapable of carrying out their work.

In management terms short term persistent absences are difficult. Some employees are more ill than others. Some have persistent illnesses which lead to frequent absences (e.g. migraine). Some conditions like this could be considered a disability (e.g. asthma). Employers should encourage employees with conditions of this kind to take medical advice at an early stage. It may also be feasible for employers to encourage staff whose illnesses are not linked to tackle their ill-health and attend more regularly.

What steps must an employer take?

Tribunals expect employers to be able to demonstrate in cases of dismissal for persistent short term absence that they have:

- reviewed the record, the number of absences and the periods of good attendance in between;
- considered the nature of the illnesses;
- considered whether there could be an underlying condition and sought a medical opinion if this seems appropriate;
- interviewed the employee personally and explained the difficulties for the employer including the impact on other staff;
- followed any workplace policy which should cover the above steps and provide for a series of staged warnings;
- couched warnings in appropriate language – employees should not be disciplined for being sick;
- allowed the employee to put forward explanations for the absences;
- considered extending the warning procedure if there is an improvement in attendance;
- considered how other similar cases have been dealt with in the workplace;
- considered alternatives to dismissal such as alternative work or working hours (particularly important if the employee has a disability see Chapter 7);
- offered a right of appeal against warnings and dismissal (which will become even more important once the new Employment Rights (Dispute Resolution) Bill comes into force in 1998 - see 5.3.2, *Appeals*).

Some regular absences mask other difficulties in the employee's work or home life. The employer should also consider whether there are contributory factors at work such as bullying or harassment or poor management. The employer will need this information in order to manage the situation adequately.

Where there might be an underlying medical condition or disability which connects all the illnesses, employers must be able to show that they have considered the possibility fully.

The inconvenience of the absences to the employer has to reach the point where dismissal is a reasonable response. The employer has to demonstrate to the employee that the level of absence, even if entirely legitimate, is unsustainable for the organisation.

Example

The case of Mr Lynock is fairly typical of a short term absence case. Mr Lynock was employed by Cereal Packaging Ltd and had a very poor sickness record which was way below average for the company's employees as a whole. His absences were all legitimate but the illnesses were unrelated. He was issued with an oral warning followed by two written ones. Matters did not improve. He was then put on an indefinite final warning. He was told that he must improve substantially and over a prolonged period and that the situation was very grave. He was then sick for two weeks and two days in July 1986, one day in October 1986, two weeks in April 1987 and one day in June 1987. His employers then dismissed him and the dismissal was upheld as fair [*Lynock v. Cereal Packaging Ltd* (1988) IRLR 510].

Policies. The guidelines set out in the cases set the framework for employers in developing and implementing policies to deal with the management of persistent short-term absence. How employers should build upon this framework is dealt with in detail in the Management Section 5.4.

5.3.2 Long term or chronic illnesses

This section should be read in conjunction with the guidelines on disability and absence in Chapter 7. If an illness or injury is clearly long-term, or if investigation of persistent short term absences has shown that there is an underlying medical condition, then different standards are expected of the employer. The reason for dismissal in a long term sickness absence case is lack of capability on the part of the employee to do the work they were employed to do. The law in this area is complex and legal advice will often be necessary before dismissal.

The cases have identified three steps which it is vital for the employer to take:

- ascertain the medical position;
- consult with the employee;
- consider alternative work or alternative arrangements for work.

The employer should also consider:

- the organisation's sickness policy;
- offering a right of appeal against dismissal;
- early retirement on medical grounds.

Ascertaining the medical position. How the employer should go about obtaining and interpreting relevant and useful medical information is dealt with in detail in the Management Section 5.4 and in Chapter 7.

It is clear that employers are expected to respond pro-actively to medical reports. If they are unintelligible or do not answer the employer's questions the employer should go back for more information or clarification. If they conflict with other information about the employee's health, or seem inconsistent with the employee's actual sickness record, the employer should not simply take them at face value but should make further enquiries.

If two medical reports conflict, the employer should have a good reason for choosing one over the other. If the choice is not made in a considered way, this could be enough to render a sickness dismissal unfair. In some circumstances it might be necessary to get a third opinion.

The information the employer can obtain, and on what terms, is governed by the Access to Medical Reports Act 1988 and the Access to Medical Records Act 1990.

Access to medical reports

The Access to Medical Reports Act governs an employer's access to a medical report from a medical practitioner about an employee or prospective employee. Should you need to get a medical report you must follow these guidelines. The Act lays out a number of rights and duties including:

- An employer must notify the individual and gain their consent in writing before applying for a medical report.
- Employers must inform individuals that they have the following rights:
  —to withhold consent to the making of the application;
  —to state when giving consent that they wish to have access to the report before it is supplied;
  —to have access to the report before and, in certain circumstances, after it has been supplied;
  —to withhold consent to the report being supplied;
  —to request the doctor to amend anything in the report which is inaccurate or misleading. If the doctor refuses, the individual can attach a statement giving their views.

Once the report has been supplied, the doctor must keep a copy for at least six months, during which time the individual has a right to inspect it further. Where an employee states that they wish to have access to the report, the employer must let the GP know this when making the application, and at the same time let the employee know that the report has been requested. The employee must contact the GP within 21 days of the date of the application to make arrangements to see the report, otherwise the rights under the Act will be lost. There are some exceptions to the act if the medical practitioner considers that access would cause serious harm to the mental or physical health of the person concerned.

The Access to Medical Records Act 1990 allows employers full access to the employee's medical records but only with the employee's prior written consent. Once the employee has given consent they do not have the extensive rights set out in the 1988 Act and are not entitled to see the records or comment on them prior to disclosure to the employer. In practice employees are unlikely to give their consent on this basis.

Consultation with the employee. Failure to consult with the employee about their health and the implications before dismissal will usually be fatal to the employer's case.

Example

Mr Laird was a security officer at an oil terminal at Sullum Voe in the Orkney Islands. He had suffered a mild heart attack and was away from work for three months. His doctor then reported that with a few more weeks off work he would be fit for light duties and would be fully fit after 12 weeks. This report was sent to the company doctor who was then approached by the local supervisor. The supervisor told the company doctor that the working conditions on the Orkneys were unsuitable for Mr Laird. Head office acted on this information to conclude that Mr Laird was permanently unfit for work and sacked him. The Scottish EAT held that since there had been no consultation with Mr Laird, and the supervisor had overemphasized the unsuitability of the working conditions, the dismissal was unfair.

The consultation needs to take into account:

- the employee's past record;
- how long the employee is likely to be away;
- how fit they will be on their return;
- whether they will be limited in what they can do on return;
- how long the organisation can manage without them;
- whether the organisation can provide temporary cover;
- whether there is a disability under the DDA and the implications if there is (see Chapter 7).

Tribunals do try to take into account that employers in large organisations have greater scope for flexibility and tolerance than small employers.

Alternative work. If a return to the original job is impossible after a period of ill-health, the employer must consider whether there are any alternatives. Medical evidence, ideally from Occupational Health, will be vital. Considering alternatives does not necessarily mean finding a completely different job, and employers are not expected to create a new job. Modifying the existing job might be enough.

Example

Mr Nolan had to give up working night shifts after a long spell of ill-health. Later his employers asked him to return to shift work and when he refused he was dismissed. The employers argued that they had no work for him because his day job involved duties he was not fit for such as going up ladders and lifting. The tribunal found the dismissal unfair and said that the daytime duties he was unfit to do could easily have been done by another employee [*Garricks (Caterers) Ltd* v. *Nolan* (1980) IRLR 259].

The organisation's sickness policy. The employer must take account of the existing sickness policy, particularly if it is part of the employee's contract of employment. It is also vital that the policy is applied in a way that is consistent with the handling of similar cases in the past. Some employers think that unless contractual sick pay has been exhausted they cannot dismiss on the grounds of ill-health. This is not the case, and the availability of occupational sick pay is only one of many factors that the employer has to consider. Employers with permanent health insurance (PHI) schemes however must take particular care in this area. See Chapter 10 for more information.

When an employer dismisses an employee who is incapacitated they must not overlook the complex rules on payment during the statutory notice period. This is dealt with in detail in chapter 10.

Appeals. The employer must offer a right of appeal against the decision to dismiss. The Employment Rights (Dispute Resolution) Bill, due to receive the Royal Assent in 1998, will change the law on internal appeals. Tribunals will be allowed to give even greater significance than at present to the failure of the employer to offer an appeal, or the failure of the employee to use the internal appeals procedure.

Early retirement on medical grounds. If the employer has a pension scheme which provides for early retirement on the grounds of ill-health, there may be an alternative to dismissal in a long term sickness case. It is the rules of the pension scheme which will determine what the employer can do here. In many cases specialist advice will be necessary. It will also be necessary in most cases to have a doctor's recommendation that the employee is permanently incapacitated from any full-time employment they could reasonably be expected to do. Employers must act in good faith in interpreting the pension scheme rules, and must take advice if they are in doubt as to the employee's entitlements.

What employers should do. A clear, published and easily understandable procedure is vital in the case of potential dismissal on the grounds of long term sickness. Many cases end up in the tribunal because of the absence of such a procedure or the failure of the employer to adhere to established procedures. The guidelines established in case law, and outlined above, provide the framework. The Management Section 5.4 shows in detail how this can be built upon by employers.

5.3.3 Mental health and stress

There are three key points:

- The courts require employers to be even more tolerant of their staff in cases where mental health is an issue. They will expect very full consultation with the employee as well as a particularly thorough medical investigation.

- Employers do not only face the risk of an unfair dismissal claim if they mishandle dismissals connected with the mental health of their employees. They may also face claims of disability discrimination if the mental illness fits the definition of a disability under the DDA (see Sections 7.2 and 7.9).

- Employers must also consider the stress experienced by their staff and must take remedial action where there is a problem. In *Walker* v. *Northumberland County Council* (1995) IRLR 35, Mr Walker was able to establish that his employers had a duty of care and that their indifference to his increasing workload amounted to negligence. This entitled him to bring a claim in the High Court for damages and there was no ceiling on the amount the court was able to award him (unlike an unfair dismissal claim).

A great deal has been read into the Walker decision and many employers fear that a stressful workplace will lead to claims from their staff. However, Mr Walker showed a clear vulnerability to mental illness in connection with an excessive workload and he suffered two nervous breakdowns. It was his employer's failure to act after the first nervous breakdown, and their failure to provide him with assistance or support in the face of clear risks, which led to the High Court action.

Example

In Halton Borough Council v. Hollett the tribunal and the EAT found that the employee had been unfairly dismissed because the council had failed to follow fair procedures or consult adequately. Mr Hollett's behaviour had become unpredictable and difficult but he produced medical evidence at the hearing that this was due to inadequate doses of medication. The council had not investigated the medical origin of his behaviour and they had refused to allow up to date medical reports to be read at the hearing of Mr Hollett's appeal against his dismissal [*Halton Borough Council* v. *Hollett* (EAT 559/87)].

5.3.4 Malingering

An employee who abuses the company sick pay and sickness absence scheme by taking sick leave when there are no genuine symptoms should be dealt with under the disciplinary procedure. Repeated offences could lead to dismissal on grounds of misconduct. There will be further misconduct if the employee produces false self-certificates. In very serious cases it might even be appropriate to dismiss summarily. However, there must always be a thorough investigation and a disciplinary hearing before steps are taken to dismiss, even where the facts seem to speak for themselves.

Example

Mr Bailey asked for annual leave to go to Majorca and was refused it. He was in fact absent during the week in question and self-certified himself as having had 'Gastric Stomach'. In reality he had gone to Majorca after all. Unfortunately for Mr Bailey two of the plant supervisors were on holiday in Majorca that very week and spotted him. A report was made to his manager who interviewed him then dismissed him summarily. The Court of Appeal upheld the dismissal as fair because Mr Bailey had abused the trust placed in him by his employer. The employer had taken the correct steps by interviewing him first [*Bailey* v. *BP Kent Oil Refinery* (1980) IRLR 287].

5.3.5 Pregnancy and ill-health

Since 1994 pregnant women have had automatic protection from dismissal on the grounds of pregnancy, or any reason related to pregnancy regardless of their length of service with their employers. In effect this means that an employer cannot without penalty dismiss women on the grounds of long or short term sickness absence where the illness is connected to pregnancy. There will be difficult cases where an illness is very prolonged, and where an argument arises as to whether there is still a connection to pregnancy or childbirth. Expert medical opinion will be essential in cases like this.

Women also have a right to alternative work if the work they are employed to do poses a health threat to them during pregnancy, after childbirth or whilst breastfeeding. If no suitable alternative work is available, they must be suspended on full pay until it is safe for them to work again.

5.3.6 Issues arising under the contract of employment

The employee's contract supplements the statutory and common law rights outlined above and the employee will have a separate claim for breach of contract and possibly wrongful dismissal if the employer does not comply with the contract. A claim for breach of contract could arise if the employee is not paid the correct amount of contractual sick pay. This could also lead to a claim for unlawful deduction from wages under Part II of the ERA.

A wrongful dismissal claim could arise if the employee argued that the employer had not followed contractual sickness dismissal procedures. The claim would be for compensation for the pay which would have been received had the employee remained in post whilst the proper procedures were followed.

What should the contract cover

A clause in the contract dealing with sick pay and sick leave should cover at least the following points:

- how much sick pay the employer will pay, for what periods and after what qualifying periods;
- what notification of sickness the employer expects including the expected timing and the person who should be notified e.g. personnel staff or the line manager;
- the employer's requirements for sickness certification;
- whether occupational sick pay will be withheld if the notification or sickness certification procedures are not properly followed - (it is important to specify this or withholding pay may be challenged as an unlawful deduction);
- a right for the employer to obtain medical reports, and the agreement of the employee to submit to medical examinations at the employer's request and at the employer's expense;
- the right of the employer to offset any SSP or state benefit entitlements received by the employee against occupational sick pay.

Generally SSP cannot be withheld by employers (see Section 5.3.8).

Frustration of the contract. Long term ill-health can in some circumstances frustrate a contract of employment by preventing it being performed. This means that there is no need for a dismissal or a resignation because the frustrating event brings the contract to an end automatically. It is difficult for an employer to judge whether a particular event might have frustrated a contract, and the consequences if the employer miscalculates could be very expensive. It is safer for the employer to follow correct procedures and to expressly terminate the contract if that is the only alternative.

5.3.7 Sickness absence coinciding with disciplinary action

It can happen that staff go off sick after they have been requested to attend disciplinary hearings. The common reason is stress, related to the events. This may be reasonable, but it need not prevent employers proceeding with disciplinary action. The steps to take would be:

- find out about the likely length of the absence;
- inform the employee of the nature of the disciplinary charge, the disciplinary procedure and the date for the meeting, investigation or hearing;
- establish their likely attendance.

If the employee seems likely to attend on the date set, proceed with the arrangements. If they do not turn up on the day, it would be reasonable to reschedule once, taking into account their likely return date. If they miss the second date for the disciplinary meeting, then it would be reasonable to proceed without them being there, provided that the employer has warned them that this would happen.

If the outcome is likely to be dismissal, every effort should be made to get their attendance or to get written statements before proceeding to dismissal. The employer can also invite an employee to send a representative to a disciplinary hearing where their personal attendance is not possible because of sickness.

5.3.8 Statutory Sick Pay (SSP)

This section aims to give a basic understanding of how the system of SSP works. It is essential that all employers are familiar with the details of the legislation and provide adequate information to their staff.

Employers are advised to obtain a copy of the DSS *Employer's Manual on Statutory Sick Pay*, CA30 (April 1997). It is good practice to give each employee a current copy of the leaflets *Statutory Sick Pay – Check Your Rights* (N1 244) and *An Employee's Guide to Statutory Sick Pay* (NI 245). The leaflets and manuals may be obtained from your local Contributions Agency Office (in Northern Ireland the local Contributions Unit Area Office) and they can also be ordered on the Order-line 0345 646 646. As the offices in England are being regionalised, the latter is likely to be the better option.

Under the Statutory Sick Pay Scheme Statutory Sick Pay is paid by employers not the Benefits Agency. The current rules relating to SSP can be found in The Social Security Contributions and Benefits Act 1992.

All employers are liable to pay SSP to all eligible employees for absences of four days or more, for a total of 28 weeks in one period of incapacity for work (PIW). Eligible employees must earn more than the Lower Earnings Limit (LEL) set each April. (In 1997/8 this was £62 per week.)

There is only one rate of SSP payable to all who earn more than the LEL. This was £55.70 until April 1998. It is uprated every April. Employers may or may not contract to pay occupational sick pay in addition to SSP.

Who is eligible? The basis of entitlement is the claimant's status of employee. In addition, the following conditions must be met:

- The employee must be incapable for work due to sickness.
- A 'period of incapacity for work' (PIW) must have started – i.e. the employee must have been sick for at least four consecutive days (including Sundays).
- Days for which SSP is paid must be qualifying days (i.e. days that would normally be worked if the employee were not sick).
- Entitlement must not have come to an end (see period of entitlement below).
- The employer must have received notification of sickness.

There are certain categories of employees not entitled to SSP.

Categories of employees not entitled to SSP

- People over 65-years-old (unless in a period of entitlement when their 65th birthday arrives).
- People with fixed-term contracts which are for less than three months, who have been employed for 13 weeks or less. *Note*: two or more short fixed-term contracts with the same employer separated by eight weeks or less may create entitlement.
- Employees with gross earnings of less than the lower earnings limit (£62 per week until April 1998). In cases of irregular earnings, the figure is calculated by averaging over the eight weeks immediately prior to the period of entitlement.

- Pregnant employees who are entitled to SMP or Maternity Allowance cannot claim SSP for the 11 weeks before the expected week of confinement and the six weeks afterwards. *Note*: within set time limits, the employee decides the date that Maternity Pay/Allowance commences. In the absence of entitlement to SMP/Maternity Allowance, no SSP is payable for six weeks before the due date, the week of confinement, and for 11 weeks afterwards.

- Employees where on the day of sickness there is a stoppage of work due to a trade dispute at the employee's place of work. Entitlement will not be affected if the employee concerned can show that they had no direct interest in the dispute, or their period of entitlement began before the stoppage of work and has not yet ended.

- New employees who have not yet started work at all under their contracts, unless they were previously employed by the same employer and the two contracts are separated by no more than eight weeks.

- Employees who have reached their maximum entitlement to SSP for this period of entitlement.

- Employees in prison, or detained in legal custody (see Chapter 4).

- In the 57 days preceding the date of sickness the employee had either:

  —an invalidity pension day;

  —a day on which they were entitled to sickness benefit; or

  —a day on which she was entitled to maternity allowance. This rule is to be abolished, probably from April 1998.

Note: SSP is now payable for employees outside the EU.

Employers' choice whether to operate the rules of SSP. For any period of incapacity for work occurring after 6 April 1997, an employer can choose not to operate the rules of SSP if the total payment to an employee whilst sick is equal to or exceeds the current SSP rate. This contractual remuneration could be, for example, wages or occupational sick pay. However, basic records about sickness do still have to be kept, such as periods of absence and how much was paid. These should be good enough to permit an employee to transfer to incapacity benefit after 28 weeks of SSP.

If an employer chooses not to operate the SSP rules, there are still some rules which must be followed:

- The employee still has an underlying entitlement to SSP.

- Adjudication Officers can still decide whether entitlement conditions are satisfied or not, if there is a dispute between employer and employee (see under the heading *Disputes*, later in this section).

- Employees cannot be made to pay, directly or indirectly, the SSP element of the payment.

- The Secretary of State will continue to pay SSP if an employer defaults or goes into liquidation.

- Entitlement to recover SSP under the Percentage Threshold Scheme will still exist, provided the appropriate details are recorded on forms P14 and P15 (see heading *Reclamation of SSP by the employer*, later in this section).

Period of incapacity for work (PIW) and qualifying days. If an employee is too ill to work for four or more consecutive days, it is called a 'period of incapacity for work' (PIW). (*Note*: The definition of PIW for SSP is different from that for Incapacity Benefit and Severe Disablement Allowance.) Every day of the week (including Sunday) counts for this purpose even if they are not days on which the employee would normally work.

SSP is not paid from the beginning of a PIW. It is not paid for the first three days on which the employee would normally have worked had they not been sick. Days on which employees usually work are 'qualifying days'. Only days required for work in the terms and conditions of employment count, not voluntary overtime. The qualifying days at the beginning of a PIW, before SSP is paid, are known as 'waiting days.'

Employers and employees can choose other days to be qualifying days by agreement, if that would better reflect the contract. This can be useful where irregular or complicated shift patterns disrupt the normal working week. The advantage of such agreements is to avoid anomalies during short periods of illness, e.g. a shift worker may otherwise receive no payment if their period of entitlement began during the 'off' week of a cycle. There must be at least one qualifying day in each week. Although there is no payment of SSP for the first three qualifying days in a PIW salaried staff are usually paid for these under the occupational sick pay scheme.

Any two periods of incapacity for work, i.e. periods of four or more consecutive days on which the employee is too ill to work – which are separated by no more than eight weeks shall be treated as a single period of incapacity for work. When two periods are linked in this way, waiting days occur only in the first period. In the second period, each qualifying day attracts SSP. This is known as the 'linking rule'. Employees are entitled to up to 28 weeks SSP in each PIW.

People who have one of a number of specified treatments every week, which means they are incapable of work for two or more days, can claim Incapacity Benefit.

Employers should remember the following

- Their notification requirements for SSP must conform to the Department of Social Security requirements, even if they require more stringent notification for their occupational sick pay schemes (see Section 5.5.5).

- SSP attracts tax and NI (see heading *Tax, benefits and National Insurance contributions*, later in this section).

- Employees may not be asked to contribute towards the cost of SSP.

- Their own sick pay schemes may need revision in the light of SSP requirements.

- Proper records must be kept for three years after the existing tax year. Such records must be accessible to an insurance officer for inspection. Failure to keep records attracts a fine while falsification of records attracts a fine and/or imprisonment.

Period of entitlement. The employee's period of entitlement to SSP begins with the commencement of a 'period of incapacity for work' and ends in one of the following ways, whichever happens first:

- the end of that 'period of incapacity for work';
- the day on which the contract of employment ends;
- the day before the employee is disqualified on the grounds of pregnancy (see above);
- the day on which the maximum entitlement to SSP as against that particular employer is reached;
- the third anniversary of the beginning of the 'period of entitlement'.

If a period of three years elapses during which the employee suffers from a series of linked periods of incapacity for work – but receives less than a total of 28 weeks' SSP – then the regulations provide that their entitlement to SSP automatically comes to an end. The employee will not be able to claim SSP again until a new (unlinked) period of incapacity for work begins.

At the end of the 28 week SSP period, if sickness persists, there will normally be an entitlement to Incapacity Benefit (formerly Invalidity Benefit). The employer must forward form SSP1, which includes a claim for Incapacity Benefit, to the employee towards the end of their SSP period, if absence from work is likely to continue. It is a criminal offence for the employer not to supply the form where required. Hence, it is good practice for the employer to provide it without waiting to be asked. Incapacity Benefit should be claimed straight away or the employee may lose money. The employee's claim then ceases to be the responsibility of the employer, and is taken over by the Benefits Agency.

Periods of entitlement (with the same employer) separated by eight weeks or less are 'linked' and treated as a single period. Linking between different employers is only possible if an employee has obtained a leaver's statement (form SSP1(L)) from the former employer, and passed it to the new employer within a week of the first qualifying day. The employee would have to have received SSP within the eight weeks before the end of their previous employment. In practice employees are unlikely to want to do this because it will lead to a loss of SSP entitlement.

Late claims. In order to be entitled to SSP under the SSP regulations the employee must notify the employer within seven days of the start of a PIW. The employee's notification may be up to a month late if they can show good cause for the delay. (see Section 5.5.5 *Procedures for reporting sickness absence*, for more detail.)

Tax, benefits and National Insurance contributions.

- SSP is taxable and attracts National Insurance contributions. This will normally only affect employees who receive other income in addition to SSP (e.g. occupational sick pay). For employees who receive no (or very little additional) income, the Contribution Agency will 'credit' the employee with National Insurance contributions, but these have to be claimed, by way of forwarding medical certificates to the local office. This would normally be the responsibility of the employee.

- SSP claimants may well be able to claim additional benefits from the Benefits Agency, if payment is relatively low. All SSP claimants should be advised to seek advice from the Benefits Agency and/or a specialist advice agency, such as the Welfare Rights Service of the Social Services Department or the Citizens Advice Bureau (CAB).

Reclamation of SSP by the employer. The Percentage Threshold Scheme took effect from 6 April 1995. It provides rebates to employers who have a large proportion of their pay bill taken up with SSP payments. Under this scheme any employer can now recover the amount by which payments of SSP in any month exceed 13 per cent of the amount of the employer's liability for National Insurance contributions for that month.

Disputes. Although the intention of the SSP scheme is to avoid the involvement of the Benefits Agency, it is empowered to arbitrate in the event of a dispute over entitlement. So, if an employer refuses SSP entitlement, the employee can request a decision from an Adjudication Officer (AO) of the Benefits Agency. If the employee is dissatisfied with the result, they have the right to request an AO's decision within six months. In the event of a further dispute, the matter is dealt with by the appeals procedure in use for other benefits. This allows for either party to appeal to the Independent Tribunal Service (ITS) for a decision independent of the Government, Benefits Agency, or any employer or trade union.

If, in the course of the dispute procedure, an employer has refused to pay SSP after an AO has decided that entitlement exists, the employee can obtain payment from the Benefits Agency. This creates a liability on the employer, the resulting debt being enforceable in the County Court. The maximum fine for non-payment is £400. Such a liability would only be pursued if the appeal process is exhausted and the resulting decision goes against the employer.

5.4 Management context

5.4.1 Principles of absence monitoring and management action

Once the legal framework to the procedures is understood, this creates certain boundaries for action. Other boundaries can then be added by the organisation itself. These can never lessen statutory rights acquired under law. They can only make them more generous. They are in part to reassure staff that the policy will not be used punitively, but also to put more human or organisational characteristics on the bare legal boundaries.

The key elements in any policy are:

- monitoring absence;
- taking positive and appropriate action;
- applying it consistently;
- setting boundaries and expectations;
- ensuring the approach to potential dismissal cases is legal and fair.

5.4.2 Senior and line managers' broad responsibilities

Senior managers have a duty to:

- know what the policy and procedures are;

- ensure their consistent application across the organisation;
- coach line managers in the use of them.

Line managers must:

- follow absence monitoring procedures with the staff;
- make sure all staff know and understand the policy and procedures;
- consult with senior staff if they are not clear what to do. Consult if the case becomes more serious and goes beyond their jurisdiction for action under the procedure.

5.4.3 How to develop a policy

Many employers are developing not only a detailed policy which is available for all staff, but also guidance notes for managers on how to apply the policy. There are sample headings for both in section 5.6 of this chapter. If you already have a policy you may want to use this section to check or review it for good practice.

Steps in introducing a policy

For those employers wishing to write and introduce a policy the following steps should be taken:

1. Discuss ideas on absence management at a senior level. Develop a draft policy at senior management level.
2. Consult on it via union or staff teams. Make clear that it is not part of the contract, but is a document to be used in deciding management action.
3. Introduce the new policy. Issues of varying the contract normally only occur if there is an existing sickness absence policy which is considered to be part of the contract.
4. Develop specific guidelines for managers in operating the policy.
5. Train senior managers and managers.
6. Inform staff.
7. Develop new administrative systems if necessary – new absence reporting forms.
8. Add to the induction process.
9. Stick to the policy, review and amend as necessary.

5.4.4 Senior managers' action

Under a typical sickness absence policy senior managers are expected to:

- apply the policy in a model way with any staff they line manage;
- train staff who need to make it work on a day to day basis;
- make sure they understand both when to act and the limits to their action;
- ensure consistency across the organisation;
- induct new managers on the operation of the policy;
- tackle causes of absence that may be to do with the way the organisation is structured or managed;
- sit in with new or unconfident managers to enable them to gain authority and confidence in applying the policy; pay attention to cases if they are proceeding towards dismissal;
- follow the procedures carefully and especially ensure all evidence is carefully collected to minimise risks to the organisation if moving towards dismissal;
- take legal advice if necessary in complex cases prior to dismissal;
- ensure dismissal is for a fair reason and follows all the correct procedures should this be needed;

- ensure the employing body is informed appropriately at relevant stages of the process.

5.4.5 Managers' action

Under a typical sickness absence policy managers are expected to:

- arrange pre-employment health checks if necessary;
- ensure all staff know what the policy is;
- induct new staff as appropriate;
- be pro-active in getting the relevant information and in ensuring that absences are reported correctly;
- carry out a return to work interview after each absence;
- communicate with staff over any period of absence rather than wait for them to initiate contact;
- have an overall picture of absence levels in their team, both so that difficulties can be caught early on and the policy applied fairly;
- determine when to start action, treating all cases in a consistent manner;
- monitor absence, reporting to central administration team, who will assemble statistics at regular intervals;
- take action in respect of an individual with a high level of sickness absence, managers will normally in consultation with a senior manager.

When interviewing staff with a high level of sickness absence, managers should:

- remind them of their rights under the policy;
- give them an opportunity to explain the reasons for their absence;
- follow any detailed guidance for carrying out interviews under the policy;
- consult a senior manager if they are at all unsure about what to say or do (if this is their first or second interview of this kind, they are expected to carry it out with a senior manager present).

5.5 Contents of a sickness absence policy

Key areas in a sickness absence policy will vary from organisation to organisation. However, a policy outline and ideas from a selection of voluntary and public sector organisations are included to demonstrate the possible variety.

These are the topics covered in this section

5.5.1 The aims and objectives of the policy

5.5.2 Principles applied to management action

5.5.3 Recruitment: pre-employment checks

5.5.4 Induction and probation

5.5.5 Procedures for reporting sickness absence

5.5.6 Return to work interviews

5.5.7 Procedure on persistent short term absences

5.5.8 Procedure for long term illnesses/accidents

5.5.9 Details of any financial benefits and insurances available to staff via the organisation

5.5.10 Appeal process

Each section comments first on the sort of information to include, then gives an example from a policy.

5.5.1 Aims and objectives

The policy needs to include a statement of its aim and purpose, why such a policy is needed and the importance of striking a balance between an employee's welfare and safeguarding the service delivery of the organisation.

Examples

Or

The aim of this policy is to ensure good management practice and to provide an equitable and consistent method of dealing sympathetically with an employee's sickness absence. These policies and procedures aim to ensure that a reasonable balance is found between considering an employee's welfare and securing the efficiency and consistency of our organisation's service.

Sickness can happen to any member of staff at any time, and can be physical or mental. Your employer has a duty, responsibility and commitment to provide support and advice to ensure you are fit to work. Part of this support includes sick pay, which is provided subject to certain conditions. In order to ensure that the policy is applied fairly, the following guidelines explain your rights and obligations.

5.5.2 Principles applied to management action

Information in this section needs to include the following issues:

- what category of employees it applies to from when;
- how it will be applied equitably;
- responsibilities of staff and managers;
- confidentiality of the process of investigation;
- communication with staff when they are absent;
- legal parameters, for example, ACAS guidelines and Medical Reports Act;
- medical investigation procedures;
- the differences between misconduct and absence due to illness;
- principles of appeal.

Example

Organisation A

- This policy applies to all permanent staff and to temporary and fixed-term staff working for six months or more. All staff to whom it applies will be given a copy of the policy when they start work.
- Where an employee has a high level of sickness absence during their probationary period, the Probationary Assessment Procedure will take precedence over this procedure. High absence levels will be taken into consideration when a manager decides whether a new member of staff should be confirmed in their post.
- Temporary and fixed-term staff working for between three and six months will have statutory rights to sick pay.
- All staff are required to follow sickness reporting procedures and may be subject to return to work interviews and management action dealing with high levels of sickness absence.
- Staff may be aware that action is not normally taken before a certain number of days have been accumulated in each leave year. To regard this as a 'free' off or as an entitlement regardless of whether they are ill or not, is wrong. Staff are entitled to time off sick when they are genuinely ill, not as an additional form of annual leave. This is one reason why managers will discuss every period of absence with the employee as it occurs.

- In dealing with cases under this policy, managers may become aware of sensitive medical or personal information. It is the manager's responsibility to ensure that this information is kept confidential. They shall only disclose it to the director, who will decide if there are other management staff with a genuine need to know. Wherever possible, the manager will discuss this matter with the employee to whom the information refers and gain their permission prior to disclosure to other staff.

- The arrangement of sickness absence is the responsibility of the line manager and should be carried out in a reasonable, fair and equitable manner. Training will be provided to ensure good practice.

- All proceedings under the policy will comply with the practice recommended or required by the Advisory, Conciliation and Arbitration Services (ACAS), the Access to Medical Reports Act 1988 and the Employment Rights Act 1996.

- The organisation has the right to medical evidence in the form of a doctor's report, report from occupational health expert etc.. Should management require such information management will inform the employee first. All employees have the right to withhold consent to a report from their GP being provided for occupational health purposes. This right will be respected. When it is exercised, managers will be required to make judgments in the absence of information.

- Management may at any time require a staff member who is unable to perform their duties owing to ill-health to be examined by a company doctor. Expenses occurred in connection with the provision of medical reports will be met by the organisation.

- A staff member's sickness absence level will cause concern if it is significantly higher than the average absence level for employees working a similar pattern of hours and it is impacting on the service of the team.

- Where an employee's level of absence gives cause for concern, the reasons for the absence will be fully investigated to the appropriate degree and each case will be treated according to the individual circumstances.

- Absence due to genuine ill-health is not misconduct, and is thus subject to sickness procedures, not disciplinary procedures. However, disciplinary procedures may be invoked, for example, where an employee:

  —has reported sick and been given sick leave when they were not sick;

  —has persistent absences from work on uncertified sick leave;

  —is fit to return to work after a period of absence and fails to return;

  —fails to follow the sickness reporting procedures without good reason, knowingly supplies incorrect information, or fails to co-operate in carrying out the policy.

- No employee will be dismissed due to incapability before: their case has been fully investigated; they have been given warnings and guidance; they have had the opportunity to improve their attendance; and, where appropriate, the feasibility of redeployment has been considered.

- Staff may appeal against action taken under this policy using the appeal mechanism.

5.5.3 Recruitment: pre-employment health checks

Information on pre-employment health checks to include: when are they relevant, when to do them, what sort of information to look for, what to do about it:

Example

(Note: that the following organisation has a particular relationship with an Occupational Health Assessment service.)

- It is important, when compiling job descriptions, to ensure that any physical requirements specified are essential to the post.

- The physical demands of a job should be clearly indicated on the person specification, understood by the recruiting officers and explained to all applicants.

- Once the interview panel has identified a successful candidate, Personnel will be asked to make a conditional offer of employment pending a number of employment checks and a satisfactory health assessment.

- The successful candidate will be asked to complete a health questionnaire and return it in a sealed envelope to the Occupational Health Services (OHS).

- OHS will assess the responses and communicate to us the outcome of the assessment. This will indicate the person's fitness for the proposed job.

- OHS will invite all applicants for paid employment to a meeting for an initial health interview prior to their appointment and for volunteers prior to their starting work. This interview is designed to explain any work related health hazards and to identify what action is required in terms of immunisations, eye tests for VDU work, and appropriate advice in relation to work related health issues. An offer of work will be conditional on attendance at this meeting.

- Where further information is required, the individual may be invited for medical examination by OHS, but in no circumstances will detailed information be communicated to the organisation. The information communicated to the organisation will only indicate fitness or otherwise of the proposed candidate for the post.

- The health questionnaire does not ask direct questions about HIV or AIDS. The OHS is required not to recommend unfitness on the basis of HIV/AIDS status.

- The organisation will make reasonable adjustments to the workplace or work activity where a prospective employee has a disability which will restrict their ability to do the job. Only where adjustments to the workplace are not reasonable will the prospective employee or volunteer not be taken on.

5.5.4 Induction and probation

The induction process should include explaining the sickness absence policy in general and what happens if an employee is absent for sickness in the probation period.

Example

- This procedure and how it affects employees will be explained to all staff as part of the induction programme.

- Employees who are on their probationary period (up to six months) who exceed the following level of absence will be informed that their level of absence is unacceptably high and will be given the opportunity and support to reduce the level. All cases will be treated individually, but a high level of absence during the probationary period could result in lack of confirmation in post and the employment being terminated on absence/capability grounds.

Acceptable levels in policies such as this vary across organisations, for example: six days or more on more than one occasion of sickness absence in the probationary period, or three occasions of more than one day of sickness absence. Differential treatment of probationers might have to be reviewed if the government changes the qualifying period for unfair dismissal claims.

5.5.5 Procedures for reporting sickness absence

Before knowing if absence is an issue in a team or for a particular employer, you need to know what the levels of absence are. This means that someone has to be responsible for collecting and analysing absence information. This can only be done consistently if the organisation has set procedures which define the rules for reporting sickness and for recording absence.

It is essential to be very clear what procedures staff are expected to follow in reporting sickness absence. There is a requirement for employers to take reasonable care to inform employees of the procedure (SSP Regulation 7(4a)).

The ERA requires that the statement of employment particulars must contain (amongst others) the terms and conditions relating to incapacity for work due to sickness or injury, including sick pay arrangements. This would include the procedures for notification of sickness absence (see Section 5.3.6 earlier in this chapter for the detailed points).

Employers decide, possibly in negotiation with the staff and/or the union, on the procedure for notification. Some elements of the policy and procedures will be there so that the employer can make arrangements as necessary to cover the employee's work. However, the SSP regulations state that employers cannot insist on notification being:

- earlier than the first day on which the employee is due to be at work (the first qualifying day) even when the employee knows in advance of that day that they will be sick;
- by the sick employee in person;
- in the form of medical evidence;
- more than weekly;
- on a document provided only by them;
- on a printed form;
- before the end of the first qualifying day (but it must be by the seventh calendar day following the first qualifying day);
- given more than once in any seven days during the same period of entitlement.

Unless otherwise agreed, notification should be in writing.

The employee's notification may be up to one month late if they can show good cause for the delay. If notification is not practicable within that period, it must be given as soon as it is reasonably practical to do so. In any event, if notification is more than 91 days late, entitlement is automatically forfeited.

These requirements relate only to entitlement to SSP. The employer cannot withhold SSP on the grounds that the employee did not follow the internal procedures, if those procedures are in the list above. For example, the employer cannot withhold SSP if the employee failed to report their sickness absence within 30 minutes of the starting time at work as it states in their procedure because the SSP regulations state the notification must be within the first seven days. However, employers are free to set their own rules with respect to sickness absence both for occupational sick pay and for management of absence generally.

It is normal practice to expect the employee to notify the employer on the first day of sickness, and many policies give a specified time (see below for examples). If the absence lasts for three days or more many employers require the employee to send in a completed DSS self-certification form (SC2) or a form produced by the organisation for this purpose. After seven days the employer is entitled, under the SSP Regulations, to ask for a doctor's certificate.

Examples

Organisation A

Notification Day 1

- All employees are required to telephone their line manger or designated responsible officer on the first day of absence as early as possible and at the latest within 30 minutes of the expected start time, unless an alternative departmental arrangement has been communicated in writing.

- If the employee is unable to telephone then it is acceptable for a partner, relative or friend to do so on their behalf. Direct contact with the line manager must be achieved as soon as possible.

- All employees should provide the following information when telephoning so that a self-certification form can be raised: name; that the employee is unable to attend work owing to sickness; time the absence started; expected date of return if known.

- It is unacceptable to leave a message with staff on the switchboard or with any staff other than those specified in the departmental arrangement. Employees who are likely to have difficulties in notifying sickness absence to their line manager or designated responsible officer by the required time, either because they live alone or do not have a telephone, must have alternative arrangements agreed with their manager in advance. A record of these alternative arrangements should be placed on the employee's personnel file. Employees who are taking sick leave must not undertake any other form of employment, consultancy work, etc., while they are absent from work due to sickness, and must not participate in any activity that is incompatible with their sickness or would prevent or delay their recovery…(it goes on to cover other topics).

Example

Organisation B

Notification of sickness

On the **first** day of sickness, telephone notification must be made to the employee's line manager by 10.00 am (or at the latest 30 minutes prior to their normal start time). If possible, the employee should telephone in person. The employee or their spokesperson will be asked to supply the following information:

- the **date** of the first day of sickness;
 - the **reason** for absence (sick or unwell are not sufficient).

This information will be recorded on the notification of sickness form.

Subsequent notification by telephone will be required on the fourth day of absence, on the eighth day of absence, and if a period of absence is to continue beyond the date on a doctor's certificate. Contact during longer periods of absence will be agreed with the line manager. Failure to meet the notification requirements could result in implementation of the disciplinary procedure.

Certificates required

- For all absences a self-certification form is to be completed by the employee and signed by the manager.
- On the fourth day of absence Form SC2 is to be completed and sent to the administrative officer. This form is available from doctors' surgeries and DSS offices.
 - A doctor's certificate is required for absences of more than seven days and should be sent to the administrative officer on the eighth day of absence. The certificate should cover the whole period of absence.
- Further certificates, if required, should be sent to the administrative officer.

Failure to meet these requirements could result in Sickness Allowance and SSP being withheld, and may lead to implementation of the disciplinary procedure.

Example

Organisation C

To qualify for payment of sick pay, you must notify your line manager on the first day of absence before 10.00 am, or as soon as practicable thereafter, that you are unable to attend because of illness. Your line manager will then inform the personnel department that you are unable to attend for work. You must also report to your supervisor on the morning of your first day back at work. For absences of less than five working days you must complete a sick certificate form in the presence of your supervisor (Saturdays and Sundays are not working days).

All periods of sickness exceeding five working days must be certified by your doctor and the certificate forwarded to the personnel department by the sixth working day. Subsequent certificates must be submitted if the absence continues beyond the period covered by the initial certificate.

In all periods of illness we may request, and have the right to require, an independent medical examination and report on your fitness.

5.5.6 Return to work interviews

On return to work the policy should cover procedures for making contact between the employee and the line manager, to discuss the reasons for absence more fully and to make sure they are fully fit.

Example

Organisation A

Following every period of absence the employee will have an informal discussion with their line manager. During this discussion the self-certification form will be completed and the individual's attendance sheet updated. For absences of more than four consecutive days the line manger should complete a sickness absence form. These discussions will remain informal unless there are specific concerns about the employee's welfare or ability to do their job or when absences have reached a specific level.

Organisation B

Managers should meet with all employees when they return to work and:

- welcome them back;
- enquire if they are feeling better and able to work;
- complete formalities such as the self-certification form;
- provide an update on work issues;
- discuss any consequences or observations in relation to the absence;
- agree any future action.

The manager should keep a note of the return to work meeting and note that it has taken place in the employee's supervision notes.

5.5.7 Procedures to take on persistent short term absences

It is good policy that persistent absence should be dealt with promptly, firmly and fairly to show that the employer takes it seriously.

Example

Organisation A

If you have frequent periods of sickness absence, the organisation may, after consultation and discussion with you, seek advice on your medical condition from your own doctor or from another doctor, subject to your giving consent and at the organisation's own expense. In addition, if you have been absent for three or more periods of four to seven days within the past 12 months, we reserve the right to request the Benefits Agency to carry out an enquiry into your case. The Benefits Agency will not be contacted until the matter has been discussed with you. (See Section 5.3.5, Statutory Sick Pay, for more information.)

Organisation B

If you are frequently absent as a result of unconnected minor ailments, even though the absences are covered by medical certificates, these absences will be considered as constituting a poor attendance record. Accumulated sporadic absences exceeding ten days in any period of 12 months will be investigated by your line manager.

Organisation C
Frequent short term absence

Short term absence is defined as follows:

- six working days or more, on more than one occasion of sickness absence over any six-month period; or
- ten working days or more of sickness absence over any 12-month period; or

- a pattern of absence: for example sickness often falling on Mondays or Fridays, or before or after bank holidays or annual leave; or
- good attendance during a monitoring period, which deteriorates when it ends;
- where an employee's sickness absence reaches or exceeds any of the above, the line manager will take further action under Stage One of the following procedure.

Possible stages for action on frequent short term absences. The procedure should include provision for the employee to be accompanied by a friend or Trade Union representative. If they decide to, then the manager should have a personnel manager or more senior manager present.

First meeting. This is a formal meeting between the employee and their line manger to discuss the level of sickness absence. The employee should receive a written request to attend the meeting, with a copy of the procedure, a specified time before the meeting (for example five days). At the meeting the manager should:

- discuss the absence record of the employee and the reasons for absence given each time;
- discuss any management, work environment or motivation issues contributing to the absences;
- identify any help the organisation could provide in dealing with the illnesses;
- if relevant arrange for a risk assessment of the workstation or office;
- go through the difficulties the absences are causing the team and make it clear that high absence rates can't be carried indefinitely;
- set a review period of between six weeks and three months;
- make clear that this is a formal meeting; and record it in the employee's file.

Second meeting. If the absence levels persist, or go down but then creep up again, after reviewing the paperwork and attendance levels; the manager should see the employee again and:

- find out if the employee has been to the doctor for their problems;
- identify any positive steps they have taken and whether or not there is any further help the organisation can provide;
- if appropriate, ask for their consent to approach their doctor for a further diagnosis and medical report, or to go to Occupational Health Service;
- make clear that this is a formal meeting and record it in the employee's file; inform any higher levels of management as required in the policy;
- set a review period for improvement (for example three months) or fix a meeting with the doctor or Occupational Health Service;
- inform the employee that continued absence will result in the matter being considered by a more senior manager at a third meeting, where a range of options will be considered.

The options at the end of this second meeting are:

- to request a medical report from the employee's own medical expert with their consent;
- medical to be arranged with a doctor of the organisation's choosing;
- a set period of review.

Third meeting. If there is still no improvement, and after obtaining medical evidence where appropriate, the manager sees the employee again. This third stage meeting should be with the line manager, the personnel manager or director, and the employee and their representative. At this meeting they should:

- go through the issues again about absence and the employee's attendance record;
- go through the medical reports;
- tell them that the organisation can't accept the level of absence;

- write a final formal letter stating the facts and the action to be taken if the situation is not resolved within a specified timescale.

Options at the end of this meeting are:

- to get medical information if not required before and now it is needed;
- to make arrangements for reduced hours or change of job;
- to make early retirement due to ill-health;
- move towards dismissal on grounds of capability or, if a lack of capability is not definitely established, on the grounds that absence levels are unacceptable. The reason for dismissal would be 'some other substantial reason'.

If there is more time needed to improve or evidence to be sought, get the evidence then reconsider the last three options above.

Referral to Occupational Health or the organisation's doctor. To be of use, the following type of questions should be asked:

- is there an underlying medical reason causing the absences?
- what is the likely date of improvement?
- when the employee returns to full attendance, what is the likelihood of them being able to fulfil all the duties of their job?
- when will they most likely be able to fulfil those duties?
- are there any adaptations or equipment that might help?

5.5.8 Procedure for long term illnesses/accidents

Contact. Regular contact is expected to take place with the employee. This should be from the line manager, team manager or personnel manager. It may include visits to home or hospital, not just letters. In some cases contact which may seem normal and caring to the employer, such as sending flowers or a get well card or visiting in hospital, may be construed as pressure to get back to work by the employee. It is very important to make clear the nature of any contact with an employee who is sick, especially the difference between informal and formal contact. The onus is on the employer to keep in contact. Clearly a balance needs to be drawn between caring, compassionate actions and trying to find out when the employee is really likely to return to work and their likely competence upon return. In some cases the liability for an accident is on the employer's insurers who may advise no contact in case this is construed as admitting liability. This may be personally difficult for both the manager and the employee.

Consult. Managers are expected to consult the employee, especially if their employment is likely to be at risk.

Medical evidence. If you need to get medical evidence of the employee's ability to carry out the job:

- Ask for written consent from the employee if you want a medical report from their GP or consultant. Consent is required under the Access to Medical Reports Act (see Section 5.3.2).
- Get a medical report about the employee's likely return to work. This should specifically ask about the ability of the employee to carry out the tasks in their job.
- If the report is not clear, you can ask for a second opinion. This could be from a different doctor, the organisation's doctor or the Occupational Health Service.

The employer may have to make reasonable adjustments to the workplace if the person has become less able. Not to do so reasonably could lead to a claim under the DDA. If an employee refuses to co-operate in providing medical evidence or to be examined by an independent medical authority they should be told in writing that a decision about continued employment will be taken on the basis of the information available and that it could result in dismissal.

Making the decision. The employer does not have to create a special job for an employee who becomes incapable of doing their original job owing to long term sickness. The employer has to decide on the basis of medical evidence whether they can wait for the employee to return to work in their original job or whether alternative work might be available. If an employee has acquired a disability but can carry out most of their work, the employer must make reasonable adjustments to the job description or the workplace.

Where the employee's job can't be kept open, and there is no suitable alternative work available or reasonable adjustments that can be made, the employee should be told of the probability of dismissal. If dismissal is the only option open, the employee is entitled to their normal period of notice and must be informed of their right to appeal. If the employee is on long term sick leave they will not be able to work out their notice period, but should be paid a lump sum of wages in lieu of notice (for more details see the Legal Section 5.3, this chapter).

An employee is not entitled to be paid twice for the same period. If the employee is getting sick pay during the notice period, whether the SSP or the employer's own scheme, this can be offset against the employer's obligation to pay the normal wages for the notice period.

5.5.9 Financial benefits

Give staff details of any financial benefits and insurances available to staff via the organisation. Ensure that details of any medical insurance benefits are available to staff (see Chapter 10).

5.5.10 Appeal process

A sickness absence policy may wish to lay down procedures for different types of appeal. For example:

Appeal against an occupational health assessment

> **Example**
>
> Employees wishing to dispute the occupational health medical opinion should produce a medical certificate disputing within ten working days from the date of the letter sent to them outlining the occupational health opinion. The case will then be referred to an independent medical referee.
>
> If findings agree with the Occupational Health Service, the original course of action proposed by the organisation shall proceed. In the case of the evidence confirming the employee's diagnosis, the outcomes or next step for the organisation will be reviewed.

Appeal against dismissal on grounds of capability

> **Example**
>
> The employee should submit a letter to the chief executive within ten working days of the dismissal, stating the reasons for appeal. An appeal panel will be convened. The appeal panel will consider the evidence put to them by the employee and the manager who made the decision to dismiss. Evidence will be along the lines of:
> * the facts of the absences and meetings so far;
> * details of any attempts at redeployment or adaptations to the workplace;
> * the outcomes of any other previous reviews on record;
> * all the advice provided by Occupational Health.
>
> The appeal will take the form of a review of the procedure used in making the decision and the decision itself. The appeal panel will consider statements from the employee and the line manager's report, and seek further medical evidence should it consider that course appropriate.
>
> The outcome could be:
> * to confirm the decision to dismiss;
> * to cancel the decision on the grounds that there were no legitimate reasons to dismiss;
> * to request further information on medical evidence;

> - to cancel the decision to dismiss and formally warn the employee that further absences could lead to dismissal on grounds of capability (the warning could be final);
> - to take other appropriate action.
>
> The appeal panel will confirm the decision in writing. The panel's decision is final.

5.5.11 Examples of organisational sick pay schemes

Period	Green Book	Organisation					
		A	B	C	D	E	F
0–3 months	20 days fp	10 days fp 10 days hp	20 days fp 40 days hp	15 days fp 15 days hp	5 days fp		25 days fp 25 days hp
3–6 months	> 4 months 20 days fp 40 days hp						
6 months– 1 year			65 days fp	20 days fp 65 days hp			
During 2nd year	40 days fp 40 days hp	20 days fp 20 days hp	40 days fp 40 days hp	130 days fp 130 days hp		40 days fp 40 days hp	45 days fp 45 days hp
During 3rd year	80 days fp 80 days hp	30 days fp 30 days hp	60 days fp 60 days hp		40 days fp	60 days fp 60 days hp	90 days fp 90 days hp
During 4th year	100 days fp 100 days hp	40 days fp 40 days hp	80 days fp 80 days hp				110 days fp 110 days hp
During 5th year			100 days fp 100 days hp				
After 5 years	120 days fp 120 days hp	60 days fp 60 days hp			60 days fp		130 days fp 130 days hp
6 years plus			120 days fp 120 days hp				
		Note: Not more than 120 days fp in any 12 months. Not more than 12 months fp sick leave in 4 years or less.				Holiday accrues during period of sickness up to maximum entitlement for 1 year.	

fp: full pay; hp: half pay

5.6 Sample policy outlines

5.6.1 Example 1

A POLICY STATEMENT

A.   Introduction
1. Principles of the procedure
2. Who is responsible for what level of action

B.   Persistent, short term sickness absence
1. Introduction
2. Informal discussion
3. First formal meeting and verbal notice
4. Second formal meeting and first written notice
5. Third formal meeting and final written notice
6. Final formal review

C.   Long term sickness absence
1. Introduction
2. Regular communication
3. Informal meeting
4. Referral to Occupational Health Service
5. Option 1 Fit to continue in present job
6. Option 2 Unfit to continue in present job
7. Option 3 Incapable of carrying out any work in foreseeable future
8. Long term disability insurance
9. Terminal illness

D.   Referral to Occupational Health Service
1. Introduction
2. Referrals
3. Medical reports
4. Recommendations

E.   Termination

F.   Appeal
1. Appeal against management action (except dismissal)
2. Appeal against OHS recommendations
3. Appeal against the decision to terminate employment

5.6.2 Example 2

**STAFF ABSENCE MANAGEMENT —
CONTENTS OF GUIDELINES FOR MANAGERS**

A. Principles of the absence management policy
1. Rights and responsibilities
2. Looking for patterns
3. Consulting with a senior manager prior to action
4. Distinction between long term sickness and persistent short term absence
5. Distinction between sickness procedures and absence for other reasons
6. Taking action – general guidelines
7. Confidentiality

B. Guidelines for managers
1. Notification of absence
2. Self-certification and medical certificates
3. Overseas medical certificates
4. Return to work interview
5. Medical opinions
6. Visits

C. Persistent short term absences
1. Absence review
2. Manager's review of absence
3. Disciplinary action

D. Long term sickness
1. Procedures

E. Appeals
1. Against management action (except dismissal)
2. Request for second medical opinion

Chapter Six

Holidays/TOIL

6.1 Balance of work/life

There are increasingly worrying signs that current pressures on the balance of work/life are not beneficial to the majority of UK employees. The trends include:

- short term working and fixed-term contracts;

- decreased expectation of a 'job for life';

- greater expectations to be available for working extra hours;

- employees' time being treated as unlimited.

These have resulted in a more stressed workforce and an increased pressure on employees to be available at all times, even during rest periods or holidays. A survey by the Institute of Management in 1997 found that two-thirds of respondents said they made sure their office could contact them while they were on holiday, while two-fifths said they would be in touch with their offices during their holidays. Nearly one-third took work away with them, and even more took mobile phones. More than half did not take their full holiday entitlement. This evidence supports the phenomenon of 'presenteeism' – the feeling that managers are under pressure to be at work and not take proper time off, because this somehow makes them look less committed or effective at work.

Another survey, by the Policy Studies Institute in 1997 for the Department of Education and Employment, suggests that career pressures are leading more and more women to come back full-time after having a baby than previously. Two-thirds of women now return, compared to less than half in 1988. Women are also working further into their pregnancy: more than one-third of women worked into the sixth week before the baby was expected in 1996, whereas only 15 per cent did in 1988.

The results of a survey conducted by MORI for the consultancy WFD (Work and Family Directions) in 1997 indicate that getting the balance right is more important for younger employees. One in five people working in 'professional jobs' said they would take a pay cut to spend more time with their families. Other findings suggested the main issues that concerned employees are:

- the employer making unrealistic promises to clients, which resulted in employees needing to put in excessive hours to bring them about;

- wasting hours in meetings which were useless;

- having to sacrifice a personal life if they wanted career advancement;

- the failure to replace leavers;

- lack of flexibility in the way that employees and information technology were used.

All this evidence suggests that flexibility on holidays and holiday entitlement is an important plank in gaining employees' satisfaction. Organisations can increase productivity and morale if policies on holidays are well thought out and consistently applied.

6.2 Statutory rights to holiday and rest breaks

6.2.1 Bank and public holidays

There is no statutory right for an employee to have time off, either paid or unpaid, for public or bank holidays, though most employers allow it. See Section 6.4.1, this chapter, for more detail. If an employer does not intend to follow the custom and practice of allowing time off for public and bank holidays, this should be stated in the principal statement of terms and conditions of employment.

There are two public holidays in England, Wales and Northern Ireland: Good Friday and Christmas Day. Other common holidays are: based on common law; detailed under the Banking and Financial Dealings Act 1971; or made by Royal Proclamation to substitute for holidays that fall at the weekend.

6.2.2 The Working Time Directive

Until the European Union Working Time Directive was adopted, there has been no statutory right to time off in the UK. However, this will come into force for private and voluntary sector workers when the Directive is implemented in UK law. Public sector employees can rely directly on the Directive to assert their rights and do not have to wait for national legislation. There have been two such cases in Northern Ireland in 1997. At the time of writing no indication of the final form of UK legislation has been published.

Once it is in place, the core provisions set out below will apply to nearly all workers.

Excluded will be those whose working time is under their own control, for example managing executives, family workers and religious workers. Action must be taken to safeguard their general health and safety, but the only provisions that will apply are annual holiday leave and the special protection for night work. In addition the core provisions will not apply to those in transport industries, those who work at sea, domestic servants or trainee doctors.

By national law or collective agreement, flexibility is to be allowed in certain areas and for objective reasons, as long as compensatory rest or appropriate protection are provided, in cases such as:

- split shifts and changes of shift;
- work at a distance from home;
- security activities requiring permanent presence;
- continuous production or services, for example emergency services, utilities, hospitals, telecommunications, media;
- industries in which work cannot be interrupted on technical grounds;
- agriculture, tourism, postal services and other industries where there is a foreseeable surge of activity.

It has already been proposed in the European Parliament that the Working Time Directive be extended to cover more of the exempted categories of staff.

Working hours. The maximum working week allowed will be 48 hours, including overtime averaged over four months. There is the potential for averaging it out over a longer period up to 12 months, if the employees agree. National legislation will cover such issues as how records are to be kept and arrangements to protect employees who refuse to work more than 48 hours per week, even when a higher limit has been set in a collective agreement.

Rest periods. The Directive specifies a minimum of 11 hours consecutive rest per day and a period of at least 35 hours consecutive rest per week. This may be averaged over two weeks or reduced to 24 hours for objective, technical or work organisational reasons. There will also have to be a rest break in any working day after six hours. The length is to be determined by national or collective agreements.

Holiday entitlement. Employees are to get three weeks paid annual leave per year until the end of 1998, rising to four weeks per year from then. This entitlement cannot be cashed in by employees. It is not yet clear if national legislation will allow employers to insist on any qualifying length of service for this leave. There appear to be two possibilities: some form of accrual of length of service or a minimum qualifying period.

The holiday provision is the one element of the Directive which is non-negotiable.

Night and shift workers

Night is defined as being of not less than seven hours and must include the period of 12 midnight to 5.00 am. A night worker is one who works at least three hours during the night, or who is likely to work a certain proportion of their hours during night time.

- There should be an average maximum of eight hours per shift in any 24 hours.

  (This may be able to be negotiated with employees and averaged over a certain period yet to be announced in national legislation.)

- For night workers performing physically or mentally demanding work, there should be a limit of eight hours in any 24 hour period.

- There may be a right to health assessment before starting night work and at regular intervals after that; also the right to transfer to appropriate day work on medical grounds where possible.

- Records of working time and averages over the relevant averaging period will have to be kept.

6.3 Time Off In Lieu (TOIL)

TOIL is not holiday, but staff often accumulate it to take with holiday or instead of holiday, so it is included in this chapter.

By law, overtime cannot be required unless it is included in the principal statement of terms and conditions of employment, along with any arrangements for overtime pay. Unless the contract specifies it, there is no implied duty on an employee to work overtime even when it is really necessary. If overtime is not paid, the contract should state:

- whether time off in lieu is to be given; if so
- how much time can be accumulated;
- whether TOIL has to be taken within a fixed period;
- what arrangements have to be made with a manager before taking TOIL.

It is very important to remember that employers have a duty of care to employees. Insisting that they work substantial amounts of unpaid overtime and then restricting when TOIL can be taken could lead to stress building up among employees. All TOIL arrangements must be managed very carefully. Even where it seems that the employee wants to do the extra hours, the employer has a legal responsibility not to let it get out of control.

The sample contract clause quoted below is from the model contract of employment in Sandy Adirondack's and James Sinclair Taylor's book, the *Voluntary Sector Legal Handbook* (1997) Directory of Social Change.

Example

There is no payment for overtime and you are not expected to work for more than 35 hours per week. When more than 35 hours are worked, the additional hours should be taken as Time Off In Lieu (TOIL) within one month. TOIL not taken within one month can be carried forward only with the written agreement of the employer. TOIL should be arranged in consultation with other staff and your line manager. If regular overtime working seems necessary this should be discussed as a matter of urgency with your manager.

Or   You are expected to work a minimum of 35 hours per week plus such additional hours as are needed to meet the organisation's objectives (or whatever). There is no payment for overtime and TOIL is not normally given.

It is obviously important to guard against a build up of institutionalised overtime which could potentially result in stress.

Certain organisations have specific problems with staff being able to take holidays and TOIL, particularly staff in small departments or highly specialised staff. For example, theatre technicians who are needed for every performance and have to supervise maintenance work may not be easy to release. If not managed properly, this can lead to low morale and poor health. See section on planning staffing levels, Chapter 1.5.2.

The following detailed clause is from a voluntary sector project with 200 staff

There is no additional payment for additional hours worked. However, additional hours may be necessary from time to time, in which case you will be expected to co-operate. If it is necessary for you to work hours additional to those required in your contract, you should inform your line manger and arrange to take time off at a mutually agreed time. You may not accumulate a credit of more than 15 hours time off in lieu at any time except with the express permission of the chief executive or a director. Time off in lieu will only be allowed if it has been agreed in advance with your line manager.

The following specific time off in lieu is normally granted:

Activity	TOIL
Training, conferences, visit	None
Residential Project Work	
less than 2 day	one-half-day
2–3 days	1 day
3–5 days	2 days
Weekends	day for day
Line managers on residentials	Hour for hour on duty
Evening work	Hour for hour

A clear agreement should be reached with your line manager before TOIL is requested. This should be authorised by your line manager and recorded on a Leave Request Form.

6.4 Management issues

The Employment Rights Act 1996 requires that all references to holidays in the principal statement must be detailed enough to allow employees to calculate their entitlement. All points in the paragraphs below must be detailed in the principal statement if managers want them to apply in their organisation. Examples are included in most of the following sections of wording from contracts taken from the voluntary and public sectors.

6.4.1 Public and bank holidays

Although there is no legal requirement to give paid time off for bank or public holidays, most organisations follow the standard pattern of eight days bank and public holidays. Some who are funded by the local authority also add on two extra statutory holidays a year, making ten in all.

Most bank holidays fall on a Monday. Part-time staff have a pro rata bank holiday entitlement regardless of whether the bank holiday falls on their working day or not (see Section 6.4.9 on part-time staff in this chapter, and further information in Chapter 3 on atypical workers). Staff who have to work on bank holidays to ensure continuity of service are often given extra pay or TOIL for doing so.

6.4.2 Amount of leave

The amount of holiday leave given will soon be regulated to a minimum of four weeks in 1999. In all employers we surveyed, 20 days was already the minimum starting entitlement, the maximum was 25 days. Some employers increased the number of days entitlement as length of service accrued.

Example

A   Holiday year basic 20

Holiday year after   2 years continuous service   22 days
                         3   23
                         4   24
                         5   25

B   Basic holiday entitlement is 24 days, a further day is given for each year of service up to a maximum of six extra days.

6.4.3 Leave year

Many organisations have a regular 'leave year' which has a different start date from the calendar year, and does not depend on the date the employee started with the organisation. Holiday entitlement not used in one leave year may have to be used within the first few months of the next leave year. Normally the whole annual entitlement becomes available from the start of the leave year.

Example

Your annual leave entitlement is X days for the complete year 1 April to 31 March.

6.4.4 Timing of holiday

In many organisations holiday arrangements are negotiated within the team. Otherwise holiday timing usually has to be negotiated with the manager. Employees with children may have priority at half-terms and school holidays. If there are any restrictions placed on when holidays can be taken, these must be clearly stated in the contract.

Example

You must request leave of more than two days in duration at least two months in advance. Every attempt will be made to meet your choice, but the needs of the service come first and the manager may have to ask you to look at alternative dates.

6.4.5 Carrying over holidays

If staff have not used their regular holiday entitlement in their leave year, most organisations allow a 'carry over' arrangement. This means that staff are allowed to carry over a certain number of days into the next leave year but they have to take them within a certain time period. This needs to be managed carefully in organisations where staff find it hard to take holiday and where TOIL is allowed to build up. If staff all have to use up accrued TOIL, you could run the risk of all staff taking off, say, the last two weeks of May.

The sample contracts vary: typically they allow between five and ten days to be carried over, which must be taken within either one month or three months of the end of the previous leave year. There is no implied entitlement to carry over holiday if the contract is silent on the matter.

6.4.6 Building up extra holiday time

Some staff may wish to build up holiday time to spend an extended period overseas or for other reasons. Employers may wish to consider allowing this, either by aggregating TOIL and holiday in one year or in allowing build up of holiday over two years. In the latter case, staff need to take some time off while they are building up holiday entitlement to avoid increasing stress levels. One organisation we surveyed had a detailed clause covering this situation.

Example

A holiday of a lifetime can be taken after seven years of service, and may be up to 13 weeks made up as follows:

25 days annual leave from the year in which the holiday is to be taken;
2×5 days rolled over from the year previous to the holiday year and the year before that;
the balance to be made up of unpaid leave.

- notice must be given in advance;
- leave can only be rolled over in years six and seven to be taken in year eight;
- an extended holiday can only be taken by one person in any department or region in any leave year and must be timed to fit in with departmental needs.

6.4.7 Provisions for holidays at non-Christian festivals

When most staff shared the same general religious belief, the whole office may have shut down over the Christmas or Easter period – the major Christian festivals. Now that the workforce is more diverse in its belief systems, it is less appropriate for all staff to have to take holiday at these times.

Many employers are re-thinking the policy of shutting the office over the Christmas/New Year period for all staff. Alternatives may be working at home or opening for that part of the time that is not already a bank holiday. The office may be closed to callers, but open for staff who wish to work in a quiet environment. Staff who are practising observers of other religions may want time off for particular festivals in their calendar, such as Eid, Hanukkah, Diwali etc.. Most employers are pro-active in allowing this. It is wise not to plan major conferences or events on the main religions' major holidays. Special calendars of these are available, for example the Multi-Faith calendar from Swindon Borough Council Community Development Department (Telephone 01793 463102).

A group of Muslim factory workers won their case in 1993 to be able to take Eid off as unpaid leave or as holiday.

A few employers give special extra days for those wishing to observe religious festivals of a non-Christian nature.

Examples

A   The office is normally closed between Christmas and New Year. Any working day falling between these dates is to be taken as annual leave.

B   Religious holidays for which an employee might regularly require leave should be made known to the Executive Committee within 28 days of starting work. These will be granted as additional to annual holiday entitlement, up to a maximum of three days on full pay.

C   As part of the organisation's equal opportunities practice it is possible that the organisation's three extra-statutory days normally taken at Christmas may be available for other religious festivals. Members of staff whose religion does not celebrate Christmas will be given the opportunity to use the three extra-statutory days to celebrate their own religious festivals during the leave year.

6.4.8 Ill-health during holidays

The majority of employers allow staff who have been ill on holiday, and can provide evidence in the form of medical certificates, to take this time as sick time and not holiday time.

Example

Sickness during annual leave and public holidays will count as sickness absence provided that a doctor's certificate is obtained. Normally compensatory time off will be given at a later date.

6.4.9 Part-time staff

Part-time staff should have the same pro rata entitlements to pay and benefits as full-time staff. If part-time staff could argue otherwise, for example in relation to holiday entitlement, this could give rise to an equal pay claim or a claim for sex discrimination. The European Directive on the rights of part-time workers will give part-timers statutory rights in this respect (see Chapter 3).

'Part-day' staff are the easiest to calculate entitlement for. A part-day employee is one who works a five-day week, but less time than a full-time employee. They should get the same number of days or weeks off as specified in the contract. The full-timer will get their seven hour day off and the part-timer, their reduced hour day.

Staff working irregular hours over each month or over the year. In this case an average of hours is taken over a sample time frame, for example three months, and the average holiday time calculated for that period. A check must be taken each year that this has not resulted in over or under-awarding time off.

Part-week staff. This form of working may lead to two difficulties in working out holiday: annual holiday and bank and public holidays. One way of calculating annual holiday is to base the calculations on hours as follows:

Assume that if the contract gives the:

> Full-time working week as   37 hours over five days which is 7.4 hours per day, and the
> Full-time annual holiday as   22 days (or 162.8 hours).

A part-timer working eight hours over three days will be entitled to 8/37 of the 162.8 hours which comes to 35.224 hours.

This is probably better rounded to a whole number of hours, in this case 35 hours. This means that the part-time employee in the example is entitled to 35 hours of their paid time as holiday each year. This works out at 4.4 weeks per year, which is the same as the full-time person, but by expressing it in hours, irregular work patterns can be more easily accounted for (e.g. if the part-timer in the example works three hours on two days and two on another).

The contract in this case would read:

Example

> Your annual holiday is pro rata to full-timer's holiday and is expressed as the nearest whole number of hours. In your case this is 35 hours.

Entitlement to bank holidays should also be allocated equally. This is a particular issue for job sharers and those who always work at one end of the week or the other. Four of the bank holidays fall always on a Monday, one on a Friday (Good Friday) and the rest move about the week. Those working on a Monday could get more leave than those working on a Friday unless action is taken to equalise time off.

Take the case of a typical job share arrangement where Employee A works Monday, Tuesday and Wednesday morning and Employee B works Wednesday afternoon, Thursday and Friday. When a bank holiday falls on a Monday, it would not be fair for A to have the whole day off and B to work all their hours.

To manage this fairly, A would not work on Monday, but would need to work an extra half-day in compensation, B would work half a day less at their end of the week.

6.4.10 Temporary staff

The Working Time Directive will probably make provision for temporary workers to have a paid holiday entitlement. It may specify the period an employee will have to work, such as three months, before starting to accrue holiday entitlement. Once temporary staff have worked any specified qualification time, then they should get holiday entitlement calculated in the same way as other staff.

Example for a fixed-term sessional worker contract from a local council

> You will be paid for an agreed number of sessions each month with no paid leave of any kind. However you will be paid for public holidays when you normally would have worked on such days, but were prevented from doing so because the project or club is closed.

6.4.11 Casual staff

The definition of a casual worker is not as simple as one might expect. Casual workers can usually be distinguished from other temporary staff by the fact that they are employed for a short amount of time on an irregular basis. Some organisations use **casual** to mean for a short period of time, or for a regular number of sessions, but over an unspecified time period.

The most important issue in this case is to make sure that staff who are called 'casual' are on a 'casual' relationship recognised by law. They could have acquired employment rights, by virtue of length of time working with the organisation, mutuality of obligation, or lack of breaks between contracts.

'Mutuality of obligation' means that when work is available it must be offered to the employee and the employee has to accept it when it is offered. Casual staff who work on a short term or daily basis where there is no 'mutuality of obligation' usually do not work long enough on a continuous basis to accrue rights to holidays. However, this may have to be changed when the details of the Working Time Directive are finally published in UK law.

Casual staff who work on a regular basis or on contracts where there is a 'mutuality of obligation' may build up employment rights and become temporary workers (in which case see Section 6.4.10). In cases where the regular causal arrangement carries on for a number of years, they may become permanent staff. If this happens, then they have all the rights to holiday that other permanent full or part-time workers have.

The courts have ruled on cases where there is a series of temporary or casual contracts carried out by the same person, even with breaks in between. Employees whose contracts end when the work ceases, and who are re-engaged when the work starts again, acquire continuity of service if the end result is that they are employed for longer than they are not employed. If they are expected to come when called in ('mutuality of obligation'), then employment may be regarded as continuing even when they are not actually working (see also Chapter 3).

If you know from the start that the employee is to be employed for one month or longer, they are entitled to be issued with a principal statement and will be better treated as temporary staff.

Example

Your employment is on a casual basis and pay will be given for the hours you work. There will be no entitlement to holidays for the period of your work.

6.4.12 New employees

When a new staff person joins they need to know what holiday entitlement they can have access to immediately. This usually accrues on a pro rata, month by month basis, until they have been in post for 12 months, or until they catch up with the start of the leave year. In most cases entitlement is a certain number of days per month. Sometimes this only accrues after the month in which it is earned. For example, take a new employee who starts mid-way through March, and has 24 days holiday per year. They would have accrued one day at the end of March. At the end of April they would have three days, and so on.

Some employers require staff to not take any holidays within a certain time period after starting, typically three months. This must be stated in the terms of the contract.

Some employees wish to negotiate over holidays already booked when they are starting a new post. The employers should negotiate sensibly and carefully over this, and get all final agreements in writing.

Examples in contracts include:

A   Holiday entitlement will accrue when you have been employed for three months.

B   The holiday year runs from 1 April to 31 March. If you join after 1 April, you will be entitled in that year to annual holidays proportional to your length of service in the remainder of that year.

6.4.13 Employees leaving

Holiday entitlements on leaving are often the subject of much dispute. They are usually worked out on the basis of either the number of completed months or weeks that will be worked between the start of the organisation's holiday year and the employee's leaving date.

If there is any holiday entitlement not taken at the end of employment, this will be paid for as part of the end salary. Holiday still accrues in the notice period as this is still paid time. If the employee leaves without working their full notice period by agreement with the employer, they will only be entitled to holidays up until their negotiated leave date. Current employment case law suggests that one day's holiday pay should be calculated at 1/365th of annual salary.

The calculation of final payment normally takes into account outstanding pay and outstanding holiday pay. In general, when an employee resigns and has given appropriate notice they are paid up to the end of the day on which they actually leave. The Employment Rights Act 1996 states that the right to holiday pay on termination must be made clear to leavers. It does not say that it must be paid, just that the position must be made clear in the contract. Contracts may therefore allow or not allow for untaken holiday to be paid at the rate at which it was accrued. Contracts may also allow for holiday already taken which is over the entitlement to be deducted from the final payments. An employer may only make these deductions if the contract allows it.

If the reason for termination of the contract is the employee's gross misconduct or other summary dismissal, and the employer does not wish to pay holiday pay in this case where they normally would, the contract must state this.

Example

At the end of your employment, unless dismissed for gross misconduct, you are entitled to be paid for any accrued leave not taken.

A deduction will be made from your final pay for leave taken in excess of your accrued entitlement.

6.5 Holiday pay

In the voluntary sector there is usually no question but that holiday pay will be at the basic rate of pay, because there is only a basic rate of pay. In sectors where paid overtime and bonuses are more common there may be some variation on basic pay for holidays. Some may pay an average of basic and overtime rates, some may pay a holiday bonus of, for example, half-a-week's basic pay for every week taken and paid at basic rate.

6.6 Rights of those on parental leave

Holiday entitlement will continue to accrue for those on the 14 weeks statutory maternity leave, and will count towards the woman's normal leave entitlement. For those who qualify for the longer period of maternity leave the position is unclear and should be clarified in the employee's contract. If employers want to impose any rules on when accrued holiday can be taken, they must put it in the contract (see also Chapter 8 on parental rights).

At present it is unclear what the rights to accrue holiday will be for those taking parental leave under the Parental Leave Directive. The national legislation will make the provision clear.

6.7 Unauthorised holiday and late returns from holiday

If staff take longer holiday than they arranged, or return late from holiday, or fail to appear for any reason, managers can take action under the disciplinary procedure. This type of absence may be treated as misconduct. Managers would need to ensure staff had an opportunity to state their case before taking any punitive action.

6.8 What employers should do

Look carefully through the written principal statement of terms and conditions of employment and check that what is written in it is:

- what actually happens in custom and practice;
- add in custom and practice terms if necessary;
- ensure all aspects of taking holiday and TOIL are covered in the relevant sections of the statement;
- go through the proper procedures for varying the contract if you wish to change it.

Ensure that conditions for permanent part-time staff and full-time staff are equivalent.

Chapter Seven

Disability and Absence

Discrimination against disabled people in employment has been driven by a set of assumptions about the difficulties disabled employees might create for employers. However, the idea that every disabled employee will need expensive special equipment, and will inevitably be absent from work a lot, on account of their disability, simply does not stand up to even cursory scrutiny. For example, only 5 per cent of people with disabilities use wheelchairs.

These views have been particularly under attack since the coming into force of the Disability Discrimination Act 1995. However, good equal opportunities practice before that required employers to aim to eliminate discrimination against disabled job applicants and employees. The DDA only applies to employers with more than 20 employees (but see Sections 7.1 and 7.3). Hence, many employers who are not covered by the Act may still want to follow the principles of the DDA in the way they recruit and manage people with disabilities, for reasons of equal opportunity.

Moreover, enlightened employers have realised for some time that having appropriate employment practices in relation to disabled people makes good business sense and that many disabled people are highly skilled and under-utilised. The problems employers perceive in employing disabled people may in fact be more imagined than real. The low rate of employment among disabled people has the effect of excluding from the workforce many highly skilled and motivated people with much to contribute.

There are a number of studies which compare the absence rates of disabled and non-disabled employees that would seem to indicate that the absence rates of disabled workers are generally not significantly higher than those of able bodied workers. One such study, undertaken by Dr Melvin Kettle of Bradford University for the Association of Disabled Professionals, found that 72.6 per cent of disabled employees had work production rates as good as, or higher than, non-disabled employees. They had fewer injuries and were absent for fewer days per injury. It was quoted in the 1994 Cabinet Office Paper *Focus on Ability*.

This chapter will focus on how managers should respond when employees with disabilities are absent from work, particularly in the light of the DDA and the standards of good practice it sets.

7.1 The potential impact of the Disability Discrimination Act (DDA)

The DDA has been heavily criticised for the inadequacy of the legal protection it has brought to people with disabilities and its failure to promote non-discrimination adequately. Nevertheless, it marks a radical departure in UK policy. Previously the regulation of discrimination against disabled people in employment had depended on a combination of voluntary and self-regulatory measures and the largely ineffectual quota system in the Disabled Persons (Employment) Act 1944.

In the year before the 1995 DDA came into force the Labour Force Survey (Winter 1994/5) recorded that only 32 per cent of disabled people were employed, compared with 76 per cent of able bodied people. It is too early to say whether the DDA will make any impact on these figures. The fact that the Act's employment provisions apply only to employers of more than 20 people has been regarded as a major flaw, as it will exempt most employers from the requirement to tackle discrimination by employing more disabled people. We would advise all employers to consider following the DDA as a matter of good practice.

7.2 The definition of disability in the DDA

The DDA protects people who fit the definition of disability set out in the Act. The definition is based on a medical rather than a social model of disability, which has been a further source of criticism. The medical model suggests the problem is with the person with the disability. The social model suggests that the problem lies with the way society is organised, which excludes disabled people. Those who accept the social model would also argue that people with disabilities are the best judge of what they are capable of doing.

The DDA defines disability as 'a physical or mental impairment which has a substantial and long term adverse effect on a person's ability to carry out normal day to day activities'. Further guidance as to what 'long term', 'substantial adverse effect' and 'normal day to day activities' mean can be found in the DDA itself and in the 'Guidance on matters to be taken into account in determining questions relating to the definition of disability'.

Working out whether an employee's sickness or injury makes them a 'disabled person' under the DDA is one of the first things managers will have to do. It will not always be straightforward. Some of the tribunal decisions summarised below give an early indication of how the tribunals are beginning to interpret the Act's definition of disability.

7.3 Liability under the DDA

The DDA applies to employers of more than 20 employees. The Government is currently (1998) reviewing this cut-off point for the number of employees. It may go down to two employees. This could potentially bring in another 1.4 million employees under the Act. Most public bodies will unquestionably be covered. However, 'employment' is defined as including 'a contract personally to do any work'. This brings in self-employed workers as well as casuals, sessionals, locums and others whose employment status might be in doubt for other purposes (see Chapter 3). Agency workers will also be counted in reaching the 20 employee threshold, and will be protected from discrimination.

This broad definition of 'employee' means that many voluntary organisations whose core staff team is below 20 will be caught by the DDA once they add in their self-employed consultants, agency staff, bank, locum and sessional staff and any others who are working under a 'contract personally to do any work'.

Employers may be liable for the discriminatory acts of their employees as with race and sex discrimination. Cases which have extended the range of circumstances in which employers can be held liable for their employees' discriminatory acts will also apply to disability discrimination.

Providers of insurance services, trustees of occupational pension schemes and trade organisations are also prohibited from discriminating against disabled people (see Chapter 10).

7.4 The DDA definition of 'discrimination'

The Act's employment provisions cover disabled job applicants and disabled employees.
Job applicants must not be discriminated against:

- in the recruitment process and in particular through the content of person specifications and job descriptions;
- in the terms of employment they are offered;
- by a refusal or deliberate failure to offer them employment.

Employees must not be discriminated against

- in their terms of employment;
- in opportunities for transfer, promotion, training or benefits;
- by dismissing them or by subjecting them to any other detrimental treatment.

Discrimination occurs if:

- without justification, and for a reason which relates to a person's disability, an employer treats the person less favourably than another person to whom the reason does not apply; or
- without justification an employer fails to comply with the duty to make reasonable adjustments.

Justification has to be based on factors which are both substantial and material. This means that it must be a real reason of some weight that is relevant to the circumstances.

This is a more complex definition of discrimination than those in the SDA and the RRA. There are many useful examples of what it means in practice in the 'Code of Practice for the Elimination of Discrimination in the Field of Employment Against Disabled Persons'. All employers who are covered by the DDA or who wish to comply with it should have and read a copy of the Code.

Some early DDA tribunal decisions have also clarified how employers should work out how to compare their treatment of disabled employees (N.B. all the cases referred to in this chapter are at tribunal level, i.e. none have yet been to appeal. This is important because first-level tribunal decisions are not binding on other tribunals. It is only decisions of the EAT and superior courts which have to be followed.)

Examples

In *Cox* v. *the Post Office* an employee with asthma was dismissed for unacceptable absence. The Post Office had a system for discounting disability related absences when deciding whether to dismiss for reasons of absence. However, it decided that asthma was not a disability and took all the employee's absences into account. The tribunal said that asthma is a disability and the Post Office should have disregarded the asthma-related time off in comparing the employee to someone who had the same level of sickness absence (COIT 1301162/97).

Mr Clark was dismissed for sickness absence which related to his disability. He was absent from work from September 1996 until his dismissal in January 1997 after suffering a back injury at work. Before dismissing him the employer obtained a medical report which said that the condition should improve over a 12-month period but gave no firm indication of when he could get back to work. The tribunal said the dismissal was not discriminatory because any person on long term sick leave would have been dismissed by the company in those circumstances and the disability did not lead to Mr Clarke being treated less favourably than staff without disabilities. [*Clarke* v. *Novacold* (COIT 1801661/97)].

7.5 The duty to make reasonable adjustments

The duty to make reasonable adjustments is not a general requirement to carry out a disability audit or prepare for the possible employment of disabled people in the future. It is a duty which arises on a case by case basis in relation to particular disabled people.

'Reasonable adjustments' does not just mean wheelchair ramps and lifts. It means an adaptation of any feature of the employer's working arrangements or physical environment which can reasonably be changed to overcome any substantial disadvantage experienced by a particular disabled person. Hence, it can also cover:

- changes to working hours;
- transferring some of the duties of a particular post to someone else;
- changing the place of work or allowing work from home;
- allowing regular absences for treatment and rehabilitation;
- providing training or supervision;
- modifying equipment.

Employers are entitled to carry out a cost–benefit analysis in working out whether a particular adjustment is reasonable.

Examples

Mrs Tarling had a club foot which had a progressive effect on her bone structure. This made it progressively more difficult for her to stand for long periods. She had been employed by her employer since 1979, but from 1995 her performance and attendance fell off significantly. The employer obtained a medical report which confirmed the connection with her club foot and then approached various organisations for advice. The advice included a suggestion that they buy a 'perching' chair at the cost of £200 (for which some financial assistance was available) to help resolve Mrs Tarling's difficulties [*Tarling* v. *Wisdom Toothbrushes Ltd* (COIT 3400/150)]. In the event the employer simply provided her with a series of ordinary chairs which did not solve the problem. They then disciplined her for poor performance culminating in her dismissal on 8 January 1997.

The tribunal concluded:

- that Mrs Tarling had a disability as defined by the DDA;
- that her employers had failed in their duty to make reasonable adjustments – they had got the right advice but they had not acted on it;
- that Mrs Tarling should receive £1,200 in compensation and be reinstated;
- that the employer should now make the reasonable adjustment by buying an appropriate chair.

S6(6) of the DDA says that employers do not have a duty to make reasonable adjustments if they do not know and cannot reasonably be expected to know that a person has a disability. The Code of Practice says that employers should do all they can to find out whether a person has a disability. The employee also has an obligation to inform the employer.

Example

In *O'Neill* v. *Symm & Co Ltd* (COIT 2700054/97) the tribunal decided that there was nothing to alert the employer to the possibility.

The tribunal decided in the case that Ms O'Neill's chronic fatigue syndrome or ME is a disability. However the tribunal decided that the employer had not discriminated against Ms O'Neill by sacking her on 3 December 1996, three months after her employment began. The reason the employer gave was that she had taken 15 days sick leave in that period. Ms O'Neill claimed that the dismissal was discriminatory because she was suffering from ME and that the employer should have altered her working hours to accommodate her illness. The tribunal found that the employer did not know about the ME and did not dismiss her because of it but because of the amount of time off she had taken.

The lesson of the case is that disabled employees should expressly tell their employers if they have, or might have, a disability. Sometimes the circumstances will be enough to put the employer on notice and require the employer to take positive steps to find out more, but employees should not rely on this being the case for them.

7.6 Managing absences of employees with disabilities

The DDA may restrict an employer's freedom to respond to the absences of disabled people where the absence is in some way linked to a person's disability. The key question is how far employers can:

- call disabled people to account for absences and issue warnings;
- dismiss them for incapability;
- subject them to some other detrimental treatment (such as passing over for promotion or restricting access to training) on account of a poor absence record.

The short answer is that an employer can do these things, but only by following the usual rules of good practice and in addition within the framework set out by the DDA. A disabled person may have absence levels that are beyond the bounds of what is generally acceptable for the employer. However before the employer decides to take any action they must ask:

- Is this a person who is protected by the DDA?
- Would the action being considered be discriminatory in that the employer is treating this person differently for a reason connected to their disability? For example, is the employer

being less tolerant of this person's levels of absence because the time off is for a reason that the employer generally has difficulty with, such as alternative medical treatments?

- Are there any reasonable adjustments that the employer can make? For example, could the employer allow more absences than normal (within sensible limits), or reduce working hours, or transfer duties to another employee?
- If reasonable adjustments have been ruled out, or if action is planned that could be discriminatory, can the employer justify it?

For a checklist when the absence level could lead to dismissal, see below.

7.7 Policy issues

Will employers need a policy for the management of absence where there is a link to a person's disability? Employers who are covered by the DDA, and those who wish to follow its provisions voluntarily for reasons of good practice, will in most cases need a policy for the recruitment and management of employees with disabilities. This section looks specifically at how such a policy should deal with absence issues and not with the broader issues raised by the DDA.

In relation to absence management issues the policy ought to be detailed enough to give guidance to managers in the following areas.

7.7.1 Recruitment

Employers may assume that a person with disabilities will be absent more frequently than able bodied colleagues. This assumption is likely to lead to breaches of the DDA.

Pre-employment health screening. Pre-employment health screening is clearly an issue. Should it be required and if so of whom and on what grounds? (See also Chapter 5.)

Pre-employment medical screening may in fact be a poor predictor of likely absence rates in the future. Barclays Bank had come to this conclusion when it discontinued medical screening for new recruits with disabilities or health problems in 1993. Research had shown that there was no link between absence levels and pre-employment declarations of disability or sickness and that in fact disabled employees had an average of eight days absence over the period of the research compared to ten days for non-disabled staff. The screening was largely discontinued with no adverse impact on levels of absence.

Equally the employer must decide whether to carry out an assessment of the likely future impact of a person's disability, and whether this factor can justifiably weigh in recruitment decisions.

It is in fact very difficult even for medical experts to predict the future impact of a disability. There is a danger for the employer in rejecting someone because of fears that the disability may have an impact in the future. A tribunal might not consider that this was substantial enough to justify rejecting a disabled person who might otherwise have got the job. Fears about levels of absenteeism, for example, might well not justify the discrimination whilst fears about health and safety risks such as the recurrence of a stroke might.

Any decision not to appoint a disabled person because of likely future developments must be taken in the light of the best possible medical information and after careful consideration by the employer of the reasons for the concern about future capability. The employer should also have considered reasonable adjustments (see below).

Example

An early DDA decision in *Sandy* v. *Hampshire Constabulary* involved a man who was registered disabled due to a back problem and partial hearing loss. He applied for a permanent post with Hampshire Constabulary after working for 13 months on temporary contracts, during which he had had five days sick leave unrelated to his disabilities. He was offered the job subject to a medical and his GP's report gave him the all clear. However, the force's medical officer declared him unfit for work and said that his back problem would give rise to unacceptable absence levels. The job offer was withdrawn. The tribunal found that Mr Sandy had been unlawfully discriminated

> against. The force's discrimination was not justified because it had relied on a medical report which was evidently 'arbitrary and speculative' having been made without reference to the actual sickness record, in conflict with the GP's opinion and without medically examining the applicant (COIT 3101118/97).

Consideration of reasonable adjustments. If the recruitment process reveals that there could be a problem with attending work on the same basis and for the same hours as other members of staff, the employer has to consider whether reasonable adjustments might solve the problem. The DDA is aiming to get employers to adjust their expectations of disabled people by not asking 'Is this person fit to do the job?' but asking 'What adjustments could I make to enable this person to do the job?'

Adjustments to working hours are an obvious example of the way in which an employer could enable a disabled person to take up a job. Flexible hours might support the applicant's need to obtain regular medical treatment; a later starting time could facilitate the disabled applicant's travel arrangements. It is a question of emphasis, and of the employer not saying 'I cannot employ X because I won't be able to rely on X getting to work on time', but saying instead ' If I make X's official starting time later and allow X to work flexible hours then X will be able to do this job'.

Clearly, flexible hours will not be an option in all jobs. If the employer has a material and substantial reason to refuse flexible working, the refusal to make the adjustment would probably be justified. For example, a management or supervisory role might require the physical presence of the manager throughout the normal working week for operational or safety reasons.

7.7.2 Medical information

An employer will need to obtain medical evidence if a person's disability is expected to, or has had, an impact on performance or attendance levels. This might arise:

- at the recruitment stage (see pre-employment health checks Section 7.7.1);
- when a disability occurs or develops during the course of employment;
- when it is unclear whether a condition amounts to a disability;
- when a condition is unstable or worsens;
- when a condition is terminal.

An employer seeking medical information should ask only for information about the person's ability to do the job. Employers should also remember that a medical declaration that a person is 'unfit for work' may have been made on the basis of the person's job before the employer had implemented any reasonable adjustments. A declaration that an employee is unfit for work does not exonerate the employer from the need for any further thought about how adjustments might be made.

It is a matter for the employer's own judgement whether information should be sought from the employee's own doctor or the Occupational Health Service. If the person is already being seen regularly by a medical specialist, it will make more sense to seek information from there. If a person has a history of disability but is not currently under medical care then Occupational Health might be more appropriate.

Whoever is approached, the employer should be very clear about what information is needed and why. The employer should:

- describe the job and working conditions;
- ask for confirmation that the person is currently suffering from a disability;
- ask whether the person is currently able to do the job and, if not, when the person might be able to do it;
- if the person will never be able to do this job, ask whether there are any adjustments the employer could make that would enable the person to do it;
- if not, ask whether there is any other work the person is able to do;
- ask whether the person's condition is stable and the implications if it is not.

Medical reports are not always easy to interpret. If the information is unclear the employer should consider:

- asking for clarification;
- getting a second or third opinion.

7.7.3 Managing changes in an employee's condition

The condition giving rise to an employee's disability might not be stable. If there is a sudden increase in absences or a drop in performance, the employer should take steps to find out the reason. This might mean a further medical report. If the condition has deteriorated, there might be further reasonable adjustments that the employer can make to enable the employee to keep on working. This has to be considered before any conclusions are reached about the employee's continuing suitability for the post.

Where a condition is progressive, the employer will need to consult with the employee on a regular basis and regularly monitor the effectiveness of any adjustments.

7.7.4 Concerns which could lead to dismissal

There may come a point where an employee's absences from work or deterioration in performance have become unsustainable and even the most reasonable employer cannot any longer be expected to make any further changes to accommodate them.

The checklist an employer needs to follow before dismissing a disabled person for incapability is not substantially different from that for long term sickness absence. The risks of getting it wrong, however, are greater because the employer not only risks a claim of unfair dismissal but also a claim of discrimination under the DDA – which carries potentially unlimited compensation.

Five main steps to potential dismissal

- If the employer has not already done so, consider whether the employee has a disability as defined by the DDA, using medical information as appropriate (see Section 7.7.2).

- If the employee is disabled, consider the employee's job in detail and whether any, or any further reasonable adjustments could be made to enable the employee to carry on working.

- Carry out cost–benefit analysis to see whether the benefit of the adjustment to the employee outweighs the cost to the employer. The suggested benchmark is whether the adjustment could be achieved for less than the cost of recruiting and training a replacement.

- If there are no further adjustments that are reasonable, consider whether it is now the case that the employee is incapable of carrying out the job he or she was employed to do.

- Consider whether there is any alternative employment the employee could be offered and is capable of.

- If not, take steps to dismiss with appropriate notice or pay in lieu. Bear in mind that the dismissal of a person defined as disabled under the DDA for a reason connected with the disability is on the face of it a breach of the Act, but that the employer can do it if there is a substantial and relevant reason.

Example

Mr Samuels was dismissed for unacceptably high levels of sickness absence after he had developed multiple sclerosis. He was away for a month in April/May 1996, two months in July/August and from 12 September to his dismissal in December. The first indication the employers had that Mr Samuels had MS was on 30 September when they received a report from his consultant neurologist. They received a further report on 25 November in which the neurologist said that there should be no problem with Mr Samuels returning to work on a 'try and see basis. On 17 December Mr Samuels was called to a meeting. At the meeting he produced a sick note covering him to 13 January when he said he definitely intended returning to work. However, his employers then dismissed him having decided that his attendance was unlikely to improve, and that it would be too costly to bring him back up to speed after his absence.

The tribunal concluded that the dismissal was both unfair and discriminatory under the DDA. It said that no reasonable employer would have dismissed an employee who had expressed a firm intention to return to work so soon, and that the employers should have followed the 'try and see' suggestion. The tribunal also said that since no reasonable employer would have acted as the employer did, the employer's reasons could not justify the less favourable treatment Mr Samuels had received because of his disability [In *Samuels* v. *Wesleyan Assurance Society* (COIT 3493/69)].

7.7.5 Communication of the policy to all staff

The employer might have exemplary policies for recruiting and managing disabled people. If other staff do not know about them, understand the reasons for them and know how to implement them, however, the effort that has gone into preparing them will have been wasted.

It is vital that disability policies are effectively communicated to all staff and that managers are trained in implementing them. It is particularly important that new staff are made aware of the procedures through induction, and that new managers are made aware of any adjustments that have been made for disabled staff. It is also vital that employees who are not disabled are not left with the impression that disabled people get special favours. They must be made aware that they would be treated with similar consideration if they became disabled.

Example

A city council has a series of policies for dealing with disability related absences.

Two kinds of leave are offered to disabled employees: (1) 'Impairment related leave' is granted where a disability is exacerbated by working conditions, e.g. asthma during periods of high pollen count; (2) 'Disability leave' is granted when a disabled person cannot get access to work because of equipment failure. This does not form part of the person's sickness records and will not trigger sickness procedures.

Medical information is sought at the recruitment stage and any concerns are referred to Occupational Health. Subject to this the candidate may be asked to a special consultation which aims to identify any adjustments which can be made to facilitate access to the job.

This city council goes beyond the requirements of the DDA in adopting a social rather than a medical model of disability and allowing its employees to classify themselves as disabled. This could lead to difficulties when there is a difference of opinion about whether a person's complaint amounts to a disability. It could also lead to abuse by employees who want to take time off without scrutiny under the sickness absence policy.

7.8 Disablement during the course of employment

It is worth remembering that only 17 per cent of disabled people are born with their disabilities. Many more become disabled at or through work, and through events occurring during their working lives. A person who becomes potentially disabled outside of, or even at, work should initially be dealt with under the organisation's sickness procedures. There may also be separate issues about whether the employer has some liability for the injury.

However, once it becomes clear that an injury has been sustained that may have a substantial and long term effect on day to day activities, the employer should be alert to the fact that there will be a duty to make reasonable adjustments to enable the employee to keep working. This is an adjunct to the existing duty to consider alternative employment when a person's sickness or injury has left them incapable of carrying out the work they were employed to do. Obviously, the employer will need medical information before this judgement can be made (see Section 7.7.2).

7.9 What employers should do

- Do not assume that the DDA does not apply to you because you have fewer than 20 permanent member of staff (see Section 7.3).
- Consider the issues raised by the DDA before taking action concerning the absences of a person with disabilities (see Section 7.6).
- Develop a policy for dealing with the specific absence issues raised by staff with disabilities (see Section 7.7).
- Communicate the policy clearly to all employees (see Section 7.7.5).
- Take all the steps required by unfair dismissal law and the DDA before dismissing a person for reasons of absence related to that person's disability (see Section 7.7.4).

Mental disability and absence: what adjustments can employers make?

MIND – The mental health charity are specialists in this area. With their permission we reproduce the paper below which describes their recommendations for good practice by employers of people who have used psychiatric services.

Positive About Mental Health: Ten Tips For Employers produced by Mind

Not everyone with a mental health problem will need adjustments to be made. However, for some people workplace adjustments are essential if they are to work effectively or even at all. Different people can find the same aspects of work pressurising or stimulating and it is important not to **assume** that something – responsibility for example – will be found stressful. The main thing is to think creatively with the employee or applicant about how to get the job done. For example:

1. **Flexible hours** for someone who needs to avoid the stress of rush hour travelling, or whose medication makes it impossible to function early in the day, can be a solution.

2. **Physical environment.** The quality of the working environment – natural light, adequate space and noise level – affects how we feel. It may be important for an employee who experiences mental distress to work free from distractions, so quiet workspace could be provided. Provision of a quiet room can make it possible for someone who becomes distressed whilst at work to take 'time out' and re-ground themselves before continuing.

3. **Organisation of work.** Set work with the person's individual abilities and needs in mind. For example, it may be better to work on one demanding project rather than several jobs at the same time.

4. **Re-organisation of work.** Reallocate duties if necessary. For example, relief of 'front-line' duties temporarily can reduce the pressure on an employee when they are feeling less well.

5. **Technology.** If someone is finding face to face communication a problem they could use e-mail; or, if incoming telephone calls exacerbate anxiety, let voice-mail take the message, with no loss of overall response time.

6. **Readjustment after illness.** Mental ill-health should be treated the same as physical ill-health in terms of sickness absence. It could be a reasonable adjustment to allow time for an employee to re-familiarise themselves with work after illness, for example by a gradual return to their full hours.

7. **Support.** Make it possible for an employee with mental health problems to manage their mental health by getting support when they need it. For example:
   - allow paid or unpaid leave for sessions with a GP, counsellor or therapy group;
   - allow some telephone calls to a friend or therapist during breaks or working hours;

- set up a system where willing co-workers can act as 'buddies';
- generally encourage staff, especially supervisors, to be supportive towards colleagues who become distressed whilst at work. Otherwise offer staff an employee assistance programme.

8. **Management training.** Provide training for managers/supervisors in adapting their management style to suit the individual giving positive feedback alongside constructive criticism and discussing needs for adjustments in a positive and sensitive way.

9. **Staff awareness.** Try to raise awareness of staff about general issues of disability and distress and to gain commitment to your policies. This should help make the policies effective and may pre-empt resentment against what could otherwise be perceived as special treatment.

10. **A healthy culture for the individual and the business.** Actively promote a culture in which all staff are valued and encouraged to identify and make changes which will help them to maintain their health and well-being, to make the most of their abilities and to work effectively. Those who have survived mental distress are often better equipped to do this than those without this experience and may be able to show you the way (see Section 5.2).

Chapter Eight

Parental Leave

8.1 Parents in the workplace

Figures from 1997 show that 72 per cent of women of working age are economically active outside the home. In addition, 54 per cent of mothers with a child under five are working outside the home, compared to 40 per cent in 1986.

In general, employers are responding with improved arrangements for their staff, both female and male. Paternity leave is no longer an alien concept. Many employers formally provide some paid paternity leave. Those without formal provision are more often using a flexible approach. Employers are also increasingly offering adoption leave, but the kind of provision varies widely. The EC Directive on Parental Leave will radically change the position for working parents of both sexes, as well as those wishing to adopt children.

In a 1997 study by Incomes Data Services (see Resources section) involving employers from the public, private and voluntary sectors, four-fifths of the organisations participating offered better than statutory rights to women in relation to both maternity leave and maternity pay.

The study showed that the most common enhancements by employers were:

- a reduction in the qualifying period for extended maternity leave from two years to one;

- an increase in maternity pay by adding a number of weeks at half pay following the initial period on higher rate SMP.

Over four-fifths of those in the study formally provide some paid paternity leave, most commonly five days. Those without formal provision are increasingly treating requests on their merits and adopting a flexible approach. Half of the sample also offer adoption leave, but the kind of provision varies widely from the equivalent of paternity leave for either parent to the equivalent of maternity leave for either.

Key points

- It is important to remember that there are different rules and different qualifying periods governing entitlement to maternity leave and entitlement to statutory maternity pay.

- The rules are notoriously complex and have been criticised by the courts. The courts have also suggested that if employers want to insist on their employees complying with the rules they must explain the rules to their staff clearly.

- Maternity leave is a statutory entitlement of all women regardless of their length of employment. However, length of employment determines how much leave a woman is entitled to.

- At present, men wanting paternity leave must rely on their contracts; there is no statutory right.
- The EC Directive on Parental Leave will significantly change the position for working parents of both sexes as well as those wishing to adopt children.

8.2 Maternity rights

Pregnant employees have many legal protections. Every organisation must have a clear policy about the rights it will give to pregnant employees and whether it will offer anything over and above the basic rights given by law. (See 8.2.6.) The examples below are extracts from the parental leave policies of organisations of various sizes. If an organisation does not have a policy, the basic statutory provisions will apply. Dismissals for reasons connected with pregnancy or childbirth are automatically unfair.

It is vital that the organisation has some plans for maternity absences and is aware of the costs, including the costs of locum cover if this is needed. The timing of maternity absences is obviously impossible to predict, but the organisation needs to be aware of the total costs involved in any one absence when it is deciding whether its maternity policy will enhance the rights given by statute.

8.2.1 Time off for ante-natal care

All women are entitled by S55 of the ERA to paid time off for ante-natal care, no matter how long they have worked, how many hours they work or what they are paid. The only requirement in the ERA is that the employee has made an appointment on the advice of a doctor, health visitor or midwife. The right to paid time off includes time travelling to the appointment.

An employer is entitled to ask for evidence of the pregnancy and of the appointment. Employers have the right to refuse time off if the refusal is reasonable. The act does not say what a reasonable refusal might be. It might, for example, be reasonable for an employer to ask part-time workers to attend ante-natal appointments outside their normal working hours.

Women denied the right to time off or pay at their normal hourly rate can complain to an employment tribunal within three months of the denial.

Examples

Example 1

All pregnant women are entitled to receive time off with pay to attend a doctor's clinic or hospital appointments and ante-natal care including parent-craft classes as advised by the GP or hospital. Evidence of such appointments may be requested by the management committee.

Example 2

An employee who is pregnant has the right to time off with pay for ante-natal care.

Example 3

As soon as you have had your pregnancy confirmed you should inform your line manager. This will enable you to attend hospital appointments on time off with full pay. You should provide evidence to your line manager of all ante-natal appointments in the form of your appointment card.

8.2.2 Maternity leave – the basic right

The basic right available to all women is to a period of 14 weeks leave (Part VIII ERA). There is no qualifying period of service for enjoying this right, and it is available from the first day of employment.

Nor does it matter how many hours a week a woman works. The only requirements are that the woman gives 21 days notice of the day she wants maternity leave to start and at the same time provides information to the employer as to when the baby is due. She must also provide a medical certificate if the employer asks for one. If she wants to return to work before the end of the maternity leave period, she must give her employer seven days notice.

Example

Example 1

An employee shall notify her employer at least 21 days before her absence begins or as soon as is reasonably practicable;

a) in writing that she is pregnant and the expected week of confinement (EWC), (the employer can request the employee to produce a certificate from a registered medical practitioner or a certified midwife stating the expected week of confinement); and

b) in writing, if requested by the employer, of the date of the beginning of her absence.

Example 2

You must notify the employer's finance officer in writing together with a certificate of expected date of confinement, at least three weeks before you intend to go on maternity leave (or as soon as is reasonably practicable) stating the date the absence will begin.

However, to qualify for the right to leave, a woman must be employed under a contract of employment. This is not always completely clear, particularly in organisations that habitually use bank, locum or casual staff. It is dangerous to assume that someone has no employment rights just because they are called a casual, sessional or locum worker. This is a difficult area on which organisations should seek external advice if the position is unclear. Some locum, sessional or casual workers may qualify for a period of maternity leave (see Chapter 3).

The 14-week period may be extended if pregnancy lasts longer than the expected week of confinement. Women are not permitted to work in the two-week period immediately after giving birth (Maternity (Compulsory Leave) Regulations 1994 SI 1994 2479).

The contract during the basic 14-week leave period. The law treats the contract of employment as persisting during this time, and the woman therefore retains her right to everything but pay. This means that holidays, pension entitlements and any other rights which accumulate over time, such as the right to seniority pay increases, will continue to accrue during the 14-week period. Women are also entitled to the benefit of any pay increases, including retrospective increases awarded during the maternity leave period [*Gillespie* v. *Northern Health and Social Services Board* (1996) IRLR 214].

Since the contract effectively continues during the period of leave, the woman has the right to return to her old job on the same terms and conditions. Any changes the employer wants to make will be governed by the usual rules concerning variation of a contract of employment. Since the law says that the contract continues during this time, the period of leave will be treated as not breaking the woman's continuity of employment. Failing to allow a woman to return to work after the 14-week leave period can constitute unfair dismissal.

8.2.3 Maternity leave – rights of women with longer service

Women who have longer service with their employers may qualify for a longer period of leave. A woman must have at least two years service with her employer at the beginning of the 11th week before the week in which her baby is due. She is then entitled to return to work at any time during a period ending 29 weeks after the beginning of the week in which the baby is born. Since maternity leave can start anything up to 11 weeks before the due date, there is an effective statutory maternity leave period of 40 weeks. This may be longer if childbirth is delayed.

The only other qualifying conditions concern the notices a woman must give to preserve her rights. These are as follows:

- 21 days before she goes on maternity leave, the woman must tell her employer:
    —that she will be away from work because of pregnancy;
    —that she intends to return to work;
    —what her due date is.

- If after she has given birth, her employer asks her to confirm that she is coming back to work she must do so in writing. The employer cannot ask for this earlier than three weeks before the end of the maternity leave. The woman must respond within 14 days or she loses her rights to return.

- The woman must give the employer at least 21 days written notice of the date she intends to come back to work. Again she loses her right to return if she does not.

The start of maternity leave. Maternity leave can start at any time after the beginning of the 11th week before the baby is due. It will automatically start if childbirth occurs earlier than this. Childbirth means the birth of a living child or the birth of a child whether living or dead after 24 weeks of pregnancy. In effect this means that women whose babies are stillborn after 24 weeks retain the right to a full period of maternity leave.

Contractual right to return. There are situations in which a woman has a contractual right to return to work as well as a statutory right. If so, she may not lose her right to return by failing to give all the correct notices at the correct times. However, the case law in this area is complex. Employers should seek legal advice if they are considering refusing to let a woman return to work because she has not given all the notices required.

Postponing the date of return. In certain circumstances the employer can postpone the date of return by up to four weeks. The employee can also postpone the date of return by up to four weeks if she is ill, but she must tell the employer she is going to do this before she is due back at work. She must also provide a medical certificate. If she does not come back at the end of the period of postponement because of sickness the employer should follow normal sickness absence procedures. A dismissal at this point is likely to be unfair.

Rights on return to work.
The right is to return to work:

- with the original employer;
- to the same job and contract (S79(2));
- on terms not less favourable than those she would have enjoyed had she not been absent. This means that she must be given any pay rise awarded while she was away and must not lose, for example, pension or seniority.

In practice a woman may not have the right to return to precisely the same job. There may, for example, have been redundancies during her absence and she may be redeployed on her return to suitable alternative employment. However, her terms and conditions must be preserved if this happens.

These are slightly different rules from those applying to women who only have the right to basic leave (see Section 8.2.2).

Is failure to permit a woman to return unfair dismissal? It may be unfair dismissal to refuse to allow a woman to return to work after maternity leave. Whether it is will depend on the employer's reasons. If the woman is not allowed to return to work she will be deemed to have been dismissed on the date she was due back. If the employer can show an independent reason, such as redundancy, and provided the employer has acted reasonably, the dismissal may not be unfair.

Employers with fewer than five employees need not take a woman back if they can show that it was not reasonably practicable to take her back to her old job or provide a suitable alternative (S96(2)). An employer of any size may also refuse to take a woman back to her old job on the grounds that it was not reasonably practical for a reason other than redundancy. However, unless the employer has fewer than five employees there is an obligation to find suitable alternative work.

Continuity of employment. Continuity of employment will normally be preserved during an extended period of leave. Other rights, such as holiday, will not continue to accrue beyond the basic 14-week period unless the woman has a contract which says that they will. It is best for the employer to be very clear about this point in the organisation's maternity policy or in the provision in the contract of employment which deals with maternity rights.

Examples

Example 1

> The employee is entitled to take in full the annual leave which accrues during maternity leave. Accrued annual leave may be taken during or at the end of maternity leave or after the employee has returned to work. In this last case the normal rules for arranging leave with the employer will apply. Up to five days of leave accrued during maternity leave and untaken during the leave year in which maternity leave ends can be carried forward to the leave year following that in which maternity leave ends.

Example 2

> - Maternity leave will not be treated as sick leave and will not therefore count against an employee's entitlement to sick leave.
>
> - Maternity leave shall be regarded as continuous service for the purposes of the employee's entitlements under the sickness scheme and annual leave scheme.

8.2.4 Requests to return to work part-time or job share

Many women want to work reduced hours after having a baby. They may ask that they share their post with someone else or commence work on a part-time basis either temporarily or permanently. An employer must not dismiss a request to work part-time or job share after maternity leave without giving the request proper consideration. In some circumstances a woman refused such a request could say that she has been treated in a discriminatory way. The Sex Discrimination Act 1975 prohibits imposing a requirement on employees that it is more difficult for one sex to meet than the other (indirect discrimination). Insisting that women work full-time can be indirect sex discrimination. Because women generally bear a greater responsibility for caring for dependants, full-time work is often more difficult for them.

However, employers are entitled to argue that imposing a requirement in this way is justified by the needs of their organisation. It might be possible to argue, for example, that the job of the woman concerned was senior and required continuity or that service delivery would suffer if the hours were reduced or the job shared. This argument might not work if the post was a less responsible one or the duties could be shared without disruption to service delivery.

The employer must always consider the request properly, and must be prepared to defend a refusal by reference to the objective needs of the organisation. It is not acceptable to refuse simply because a particular job has not been shared before or because the Chair of the organisation does not like the idea of job sharing or part-time work.

The Directive on Part-Time Workers, due to be implemented in the UK by 1999, aims to encourage employers to be flexible in their attitudes to work and to permit part-time work whenever it is feasible.

Example

> After taking a period of maternity leave it may be possible to negotiate special terms relating to your return to work, e.g. job sharing or working on a part-time basis. This will be a matter of individual negotiation between you and your employer. The employer reserves the right to refuse a request for part-time work or job-sharing where the job requires the full-time attendance at work of one person.

8.2.5 Maternity pay

The right to receive pay during maternity leave may arise out of the woman's contract of employment or out of statute or both. Confusingly, the right to statutory maternity pay does not coincide with the right to statutory maternity leave. Statutory maternity pay is only available to women who comply with the following conditions.

SMP conditions

- They must have at least six months (26 weeks) continuous service with the same employer at the beginning of the 15th week before the week the baby is due. In practice, the woman's contract must still be in operation at that date, but she does not actually have to be working.
- Their average weekly earnings must be above the prevailing National Insurance lower limit (for 1997/98 this is £61 per week).
- They must have ceased to work because of the pregnancy or in order to have the baby (there are anti-avoidance provisions which prevent employers sacking women to avoid liability to pay SMP).
- They have given the employer 21 days prior notice that they will be absent due to pregnancy. If childbirth occurs earlier than the expected week of childbirth, a woman must inform her employer in order to remain entitled to SMP.
- They must provide the employer with a certificate of maternity (MATB1).

The amount of SMP is 90 per cent of full pay for the first six weeks of the period of leave and a further 12 weeks at the lower rate (currently £55.70 per week). The period for which a woman can receive SMP is therefore longer than the basic 14-week period of leave.

Disputes about entitlement to SMP are dealt with by the DSS not the Employment Tribunal. They are initially dealt with by Adjudication Officers. There is a right of appeal to the Social Security Appeal Tribunal and then to the Social Security Commissioners. An employer who does not comply with an order from the DSS to pay SMP and who has not appealed, is guilty of an offence and will be liable to pay a fine.

An employer may have decided to pay more than the statutory amounts to all or some of its staff. For example it may offer women with more than one year's continuous service a number of weeks at half pay on top of the lower rate of SMP. It will be up to the employer to decide what rules to impose in relation to any additional payments made in this way. The scheme that any particular employer adopts has to be appropriate to the organisation's size and resources. See the examples below.

Examples

Example 1

The employer will provide enhanced maternity pay to all eligible employees. Eligible employees are those who have completed at least two years continuous service by the beginning of the 11th week prior to the week the baby is due.

Enhanced maternity pay will consist of 50 per cent of normal weekly wage (or statutory maternity pay if greater) for 12 weeks commencing with the seventh week of your maternity leave period provided that should you fail to return to work for the employer for a period of at least three months after the end of your maternity leave, the employer will require you to repay the difference between the enhanced maternity pay you have received and statutory maternity pay at the lower rate. In appropriate cases the employer may recover this sum by deductions from your salary.

Example 2

1. Payments for employees who have less than one year's continuous local government service at the beginning of the 11th week before the EWC shall be the employee's entitlement to SMP.
2. Payment for employees who have completed not less than one year's continuous local government service at the 11th week before the EWC shall be as follows:
   a   for the first six weeks of absence an employee shall be entitled to nine-tenths of a week's pay offset against payments made by way of SMP (or, in the case of employees not entitled to SMP, maternity allowance);

> b　if the employee has declared her intention to return to work then for the next 12 weeks she shall be paid half a week's pay in addition to SMP (or maternity allowance) and without deduction except by the amount by which half pay plus SMP (or maternity allowance) exceeds the amount of normal full pay;
>
> c　an employee who does not intend to return to work shall, after the first six weeks of absence, be entitled only to SMP (or maternity allowance);
>
> d　payments to an employee under (2) above shall be made on the understanding that the employee will return to work for a period of at least three months at the end of her maternity leave. This may be varied by the employer in exceptional cases. If not so varied, a woman who does not return after being paid on the understanding that she would do so will be liable to refund any payment made in excess of SMP or any part of it that her employer shall specify.

8.2.6 What employers should do

Employers must have a clear policy about the rights they will give to pregnant employees. First they must decide if they want to, and are in a position financially to, offer anything additional to the basic rights given by law.

The policy needs to cover

- how much leave;
- when it can be taken;
- what pay will be offered and for how long;
- what notice the organisation requires of the pregnancy, the date on which the employee wants to start maternity leave, and the date on which she wants to return;
- any conditions the organisation wants to impose if women are offered greater than minimum statutory rights;
- what happens if the woman needs to postpone her return;
- how the rest of the employee's contractual rights will be treated during her maternity leave, e.g. will holiday continue to accrue, will pension contributions be paid, will she be able to retain a company car;
- what rights she has under Health and Safety law (see chapter 2).

8.3 Parental leave

At present, English law only gives rights to mothers (although contracts of employment might give rights to fathers or adoptive parents).

Examples

Example 1

> Ten working days leave with pay will be granted to an employee whose partner is expecting a baby. To qualify the employee must:
> - have at least one year's continuous service at the date the baby is due;
> - submit to the employer if requested a copy of his/her partner's certificate of pregnancy;
> - take the leave within three weeks either side of expected date of the birth of the baby;
> - agree the leave dates with the director.

Example 2

Maternity Support Leave of five days with pay will be granted to the partner or nominated carer of an expectant mother at or around the time of the birth. A nominated carer is the person nominated by the mother to assist in the care of the child and to provide support to the mother at or around the time of the birth.

Example 3

An employee shall be entitled to ten days leave with pay in connection with the birth of a child to a person with whom the employee is in an established relationship. The leave must be taken within six weeks of the birth of the child unless the employer agrees otherwise in exceptional circumstances. Only one such leave period will be granted in any period of nine months. To qualify for such leave the employee must give notice in writing at least three months before the expected date of the birth together with a copy of the certificate which shows the expected week of confinement. Employees with less than three months service must give as much notice as practicable.

This arrangement will also apply to employees who are adopting a child.

However, since the UK government signed up to the Social Chapter in June 1997, this will all change. The Social Chapter has the principal aim of allowing the European Union to make laws in the social policy field, which was not possible under the Treaty of Rome. So far, two social policy measures have been adopted; the Works Council Directive and the Parental Leave Directive. The Parental Leave Directive was adopted in June 1996. The UK will have until October 1999 to introduce legislation which gives effect to the Directive.

8.3.1 The EC Directive on Parental Leave

The directive sets out two basic rights:

- the right to three months unpaid parental leave;
- the right to time off for urgent family reasons.

The main features of the right to three months leave are:

- it is unpaid;
- it is available on the grounds of the birth or adoption of a child;
- it is available for each child;
- it is available separately to each parent;
- it is a right additional to statutory maternity rights.

It will be up to the UK government to decide:

- the time limits for taking the leave (the directive says any time before the child is eight);
- whether there should be a qualifying period (this may not exceed a year);
- what special rules should apply to adoption;
- whether parental leave should be taken full or part-time or in the form of a time credit system;
- what special rules there should be for small employers.

The right to time off for urgent family reasons will give a basic statutory right to time off 'in cases of sickness or accident making the immediate presence of the worker indispensable'.

It will be up to the UK government to decide the conditions and rules, including the amount of time off in any year or in any particular case.

8.3.2 What employers should do

Many employers already offer something akin to the right to time off for urgent family reasons, usually in the guise of compassionate leave. Unpaid leave for partners after birth, or for either parent in the case of adoption, is far less common. Employers need to be planning now for these changes in the law. Most organisations add something at least to the bare statutory framework in terms of rights to maternity and parental leave, but how much is added varies enormously from employer to employer. Below are some examples taken from organisations of differing sizes.

Examples

Housing Association A

Company maternity leave:
Eligibility: one year's service by the 11th week prior to EWC
Duration: 11 weeks before EWC, 33 weeks after birth

Company maternity pay:
Eligibility: one year's permanent service by the 11th week prior to EWC
Amount: full salary (inclusive of SMP) for 12 weeks then six weeks on lower of SMP plus half pay or full pay
Repayment: return to work requirement of three months

Benefits during maternity leave:
Pension contributions and life and disability insurance cover maintained throughout; holidays accrue throughout; company cars retained

Paternity leave:
Five days paid for all male staff to be taken at the time of or after birth. Further discretionary unpaid leave. Dependant or special leave of up to ten days with pay

Adoption leave:
Available on same basis as maternity leave but flexible leave arrangements allowed according to age and special needs of the child and operational needs of the employer

Housing Association B

Company maternity leave:
Eligibility: 18 months service by the 11th week before the EWC
Duration: 11 weeks before EWC and up to 29 weeks after birth

Company maternity pay:
  Eligibility: as for leave
  Amount: six weeks at full pay, 12 weeks at half pay
  Repayment: none

Benefits during maternity leave:
Annual leave and public holidays accrue for first 14 weeks; for holidays and private health cover whole of first maternity leave period counts for continuity of service – thereafter only first 14 weeks counts; company cars retained for at least 14 weeks, thereafter according to operational needs; pension, health and life cover maintained throughout

Paternity leave:
Employees with 12 months service entitled to two days paid leave within six weeks of the birth. Consideration given to flexible working after the birth

Adoption leave:
None specified

National Charity A

Company maternity leave:
Eligibility: one year's service at qualifying week
Duration: 40 weeks for those with one year's service; 24 weeks for those with between 26 weeks and one year; statutory for others

Company maternity pay:
Amount: those with one year's service receive full pay for 18 weeks on condition that they return to work for 12 weeks. Charity tops up full pay for this category with the equivalent of six weeks at lower rate SMP. Those not returning receive six weeks full pay topped up by the equivalent of six weeks lower rate SMP plus 12 weeks at lower rate SMP. Option of receiving a lump sum payment at the beginning of leave
Repayment: none

Benefits during maternity leave:
Annual leave accrues for 18 weeks and is paid at start of maternity leave. Public holidays paid if normally worked. Company cars retained for 14 weeks only
Pension: option of 40 weeks interrupted service or scheme for maintaining contributions. Life and health insurance maintained throughout.

Paternity leave:
All affected employees entitled to ten days leave to be taken up to one month before the EWC or within seven months of the birth. Discretionary extensions

Adoption leave:
None specified

National Charity B

Company maternity leave:
Eligibility: one year's service
Duration: 11 weeks before the birth followed by the balance of paid leave entitlement (see below) and then optional unpaid leave of up to 52 further weeks

Company maternity pay.
Amount: six weeks on full pay for all staff. 13 weeks full pay and 13 weeks half pay after one year of service. 26 weeks full pay after two years of service.
Repayment: amounts over and above SMP repayable in full by those with less than one year's service who fail to return for at least 26 weeks and those with more than one year's service who fail to return for at least 12 weeks. Special rules for those returning part-time

Benefits during maternity leave:
Maternity leave counted as continuous service for purposes of accruing rights under annual leave, redundancy and sickness schemes. Annual leave does not accrue during periods of unpaid leave. Health insurance maintained throughout leave

Paternity (parental) leave:
Up to six weeks on full pay to be taken within three months either side of the birth of the baby. Available to any partner of a person with primary caring responsibility for the baby

Adoption leave:
None specified

Local authority A

Company maternity leave:
Eligibility: 6 months continuous local government service by the 11th week before the EWC
Duration: up to 63 weeks leave starting from the 11th week before the EWC (and reduced accordingly if leave starts later). Statutory leave for those with less than 6 months service

Company maternity pay:
Eligibility: as for leave
Amount: six weeks at 90 per cent pay then 12 weeks at lower of half pay plus lower rate SMP or full pay
Repayment: 12 weeks half pay repayable unless returning to local authority work (not necessarily with the same authority) for at least three months

Benefits during maternity leave:
Annual leave accrues but carry over not allowed. Scheme for payment of essential car user allowance during leave. Pension scheme contributions by employer and employee continue during paid leave. Optional contributions during unpaid leave

Paternity leave:
Five days paid leave available at the time of the birth. Male employees with at least a year's service at the EWC may apply for up to 45 weeks unpaid leave to begin within six weeks of the birth. Requests for reduced hours or flexitime by either parent after the birth considered sympathetically

Adoption leave:
12 weeks leave at half pay and up to 40 weeks unpaid leave. Leave should begin when the child joins the family. Negotiable further unpaid leave up to 52 weeks. Flexible working always negotiable

Local authority B

Company maternity leave:
Eligibility: permanent staff only, otherwise no service requirements
Duration: up to 51 weeks

Company maternity pay:
Eligibility: six months service (permanent staff only) by the 11th week before EWC for maximum entitlement
Amount: more than six months service, six weeks at 90 per cent pay (including SMP) then 30 weeks at half pay plus SMP or 15 weeks full pay. Less than six months service, six weeks at 90 per cent pay (including SMP) then 12 weeks at half pay plus SMP. Local government national conditions apply to temporary staff
Repayment: amounts over SMP repayable if employee fails to return to work for at least three months

Benefits during maternity leave:
Annual leave accrues throughout. Public holidays paid throughout. Pension scheme contributions maintained throughout. Long term disability insurance unaffected

Paternity leave:
Five days paid leave available to any person nominated by the mother as the primary provider of support. Extensions are negotiable

Adoption leave:
Permanent staff are eligible for one week's paid leave and up to 12 weeks half pay for a child below school age. Six weeks unpaid leave if the child is above school age

Chapter Nine

Other Absences

For the general management issues related to other absences see Chapter 1.

This range of reasons for absence caused less concern to the managers we spoke to than sickness absence. This is an area where organisations can benefit their staff even if they are unable to offer average or higher than average salaries. This may assist in both recruiting and retaining high quality staff.

Carers' leave is the area where there is the most disparity in policies between organisations. It is an aspect of absence which arouses strong views and feelings. For these reasons it is important that employers have thought through their attitude to this category of absence, and then communicated the policies clearly to staff.

These areas are governed by perceptions of good practice, industry norms, and contractual rights, rather than by law. The provision in the contract must take into account the size and financial health of the organisation. Small voluntary organisations may aspire to local authority conditions of service but simply not be able to afford it bearing in mind the effect of lost time as well as financial costs.

9.1 Compassionate leave

Where do you draw the line?

> A Luton policeman has lodged a complaint after he was refused compassionate leave when his pet rabbit died. (Reprinted in *Guardian Society* 12 November, 1997 from *Luton/Dunstable*, 12 October 1997.)

Compassionate leave is not part of annual leave, but is given for reasons of compassion towards another human being. Contractual rights to compassionate leave vary enormously from none whatsoever, to significant amounts of paid leave. The *Green Book* has it under 'special leave' and it may be granted at the discretion of a person in authority, to be given with or without pay. Most organisations consider applications for compassionate leave individually on merit.

Policy issues

Issues which play a part in deciding how much time will be given, and in what circumstances, include:

- The culture of the organisation concerning absence.
- The definition of the 'family'. This can be close blood relations only or extend to close friends and neighbours as well. When close blood relatives live at a distance for many employees the wider definition can be appropriate.

- The range of circumstances. This can range from death or funerals only, to emergencies, operations or long drawn out illnesses.
- Whether the employee is expected to use their annual leave in the first instance. One danger of expecting annual leave to be used is that employees may have insufficient left to meet the normal need for a break and a rest. The shortage of paid holiday may, in turn, lead to low morale, if not sickness of the employee themselves.
- The impact on the employee. If the employee is distracted or worried about people outside work, or grieving, they will be less able to work. The balance of discretion will depend on a realistic and compassionate assessment of their ability to perform to expected standards or to deal with users, who themselves may be stressed. It may make more sense for them to be at home.
- The impact on the work of the organisation. The scope to give extended leave may vary with the capacity of the organisation to manage the workload without the employee.

The policy on compassionate leave will need to include:
- the circumstances in which it may be granted;
- who is able to decide if it will be granted;
- how many days it will be;
- whether it is paid or unpaid;
- whether a form needs to be filled in.

9.1.1 What organisations actually do

Examples from organisations ranging from five employees to 14,000 suggest that:
- size of organisation does not affect the policies;
- some organisations describe the circumstances where compassionate leave will be allowed in detail; and others simply say it will be at the discretion of the line manager and decided on the circumstances of each case;
- the application usually has to go to the line manager or to the director;
- whether the leave is with or without pay is one of the critical factors. Most were with pay in the first instance up to at least the first five days;
- one organisation had an appeal procedure to assist with ensuring consistency across the organisation and a fairer approach;
- some organisations include dependants' leave or carers' leave within compassionate leave and others separate them;
- most talk of the death of a relative, which is assumed will need more than one day;
- few mention funerals of people wider than close family but still important in the employee's personal life. Where included these would take only one day.

The IDS Study *Discretionary Leave* (624/April 1997) found nearly all the organisations in the study made some provision for special leave following a bereavement. 'Over four-fifths allow a period of paid leave, usually between one and five days, depending on the relationship of the employee to the deceased. Additional time off may be allowed at an organisation's discretion in cases of a particularly close bereavement or where the individual has responsibility for making the funeral arrangements. A smaller number of organisations do not have set periods of paid time off but leave the decision to the discretion of the individual managers, who can take account of all the circumstances.' The IDS Studies look mainly at commercial companies but also some public sector organisations and a few of the larger charities.

Having seen the huge range of policies being used, our view is that in smaller organisations it is reasonable that this leave is at the discretion of the director, provided that the policy is applied fairly between individuals. This is very important. In bigger organisations we feel that some contractual leave is good practice, if the circumstances are carefully defined.

Circumstances where different organisations allow leave include:

- serious illness or death of a close relative;
- sudden illness of dependant (this overlaps with carer's leave);
- sickness of cohabitee/partner/spouse or close relative;
- death of non-blood relative;
- attendance at a funeral;
- breakdown of normal arrangements for care of child(ren) or relative(s) for whom the member of staff has caring responsibilities;
- domestic crises (fire, flood etc.).

Examples of procedures

- In smaller organisations, leave is usually granted at the discretion of the director. In one organisation 'limited' compassionate leave can be granted by the director but additional days must be given by the chair of the relevant sub-committee of the board.

- In medium to large organisations, leave is usually at the discretion of the line manager.

- The *Green Book* specifies that 'additional leave with or without pay may be granted in special circumstances at the discretion of the employing authority.'

- Most employers prefer advance notice but recognise that in the circumstances this is not always possible.

- Completion of a form may be required for the records.

Examples of how much time is given

- Up to 15 paid days in any 12-month period, in addition to dependant's leave. This was the most common specified number of days.

- Up to five paid working days in one leave year was a common alternative.

- Additional days to these specified paid ones may be allowed at discretion of the management.

- The *Green Book* does not mention a number of days and this total discretion applied to a few other organisations.

9.2 Carers' or dependants' leave

Carers' leave is leave taken by employees when the usual arrangements for care of their children or relatives, for whom they have caring responsibilities, unexpectedly break down. Causes may include:

- serious illness of the child or relative beyond the capacity of the usual substitute carer;
- illness of the substitute carer.

Flexible working provisions may cover needs for holiday or half term care of children. This is not generally included in carers' leave. Provision for carers' leave recognises that carers do have responsibilities outside work. Usually these caring responsibilities do not clash with work. When they do, the employer should have a policy to enable the organisation to respond.

9.2.1 The debate on carers' leave

Some organisations recognise that employees face a variety of demands from their family responsibilities and see this as an equal opportunities issue. Other organisations do not make this connection with equality, and have a culture of long hours with little flexibility for responsibilities outside work. It is felt that if staff take on a job they should make provision for their dependants in all circumstances, so they are in a position to contribute equally to delivering the work. Some of these organisations find that they have, consequently, a distinctive staffing profile – e.g. single people in their thirties without dependants and often of the same class and race background. Where this is the case, it means that carers either have to lie and say they are sick when they need carers' leave, or they decide not to take the posts they apply for.

In this latter type of organisation, the employer may find a higher attendance record, although this is not guaranteed, but they will miss out on a wider range of potential employees when they recruit.

Some views on carers' leave

Parents should not take on jobs unless they know their children can be cared for by others (possibly several people) in every circumstance.

I very rarely take sick leave myself, and I work very hard, but the employer must understand I am a parent too. When my children are seriously ill then I or my partner must be with them. I will make up the work as soon as I can.

If my children are ill, I will arrange to call into the office to collect work to take home to do when they are asleep.

I feel taken for granted. It is expected that I will always cover when my colleagues are absent to care for dependants and I am here as I have no dependants.

I found myself feeling angry that it seems our employee is always the parent who stays at home and cares for the sick children rather than their mother, who is freelance.

9.2.2 What organisations actually do

Organisations vary in their definition of carers' leave, and some include it in compassionate leave. In our investigations we found the most generous organisation was one of the smallest, with fewer than ten employees. There was a wide range of provision in organisations of over 100 employees. The clauses below are based closely on real examples from statutory and voluntary organisations of a wide range of size.

Examples

- Up to 20 days paid leave when problems arise with the care of dependants for whom the employee is responsible, in addition to compassionate leave. Unpaid leave can also be negotiated. In addition to salary, a Dependant's Allowance is payable to an employee if they have a child under 16 years of age or a child of 16–19 in full-time education and wholly financially dependent upon them.

- Carers' leave is included with compassionate leave. Up to 15 working days in one year may be taken on full pay, with additional days granted at discretion.

- Unpaid leave can be negotiated.

- Employees must take annual leave in these circumstances. Where this is exhausted two days of paid leave may be granted by the management.

- The director gives consent to each application on its merits.

- Children who are off-colour but not seriously ill may be brought to the office.

- Employees with children or dependants who are sick may take work home to do.

- The *Green Book* states 'Authorities should take reasonable steps to ensure adequate support for employees with responsibilities for children and dependants.'

The 1997 IDS Study (see Section 9.1.1) found 'A growing, but still small, number of companies are allowing employees with dependants (either children or elderly relatives) to take special leave in cases of emergency such as illness. Many organisations believe that initiating a carers' leave policy promotes honesty in the employment relationship because it cuts down on staff feigning illness when a domestic crisis arises. Such leave, however, is completely discretionary in the majority of these companies and may be paid or unpaid. A few organisations offer guidelines for paid leave; at BT, for example, up to two weeks paid leave may be allowed.'

9.3 Flexible working arrangements

Flexible working is an excellent development in modern working practices and the statistics show that it is a means to reduce absence rates. The Industrial Society has reported that organisations with flexible working arrangements have an average absence rate of 3.18 per cent. The national norm for England is 3.59 per cent. Flexible working arrangements complement policies on carers' leave, to enable people with dependants to work. Flexible working arrangements can include both part-time working and working full-time but not at 'normal' hours.

Options include:

- core hours when you must be in work with some choice over when the remaining contracted hours are worked;

- arrangements that fit with school hours in term-time and are different in the school holidays;

- working fewer than five days a week – part-time;

- working fewer longer days which add up to full-time hours;

- partially working from home.

9.3.1 The Directive on Part-Time Work

The Framework Agreement on Part-Time Work, which was drawn up in May 1997 has now been adopted as an EU Directive. The UK has two years to implement it.

The Directive covers all part-time employees (although some categories of casual workers are likely to be excluded but the position is not yet clear). It seeks to:

- improve the quality of part-time work;

- promote the development of part-time work on a voluntary basis;

- contribute to the flexible organisation of working time, while taking account of employers' and employees' needs.

It is too early to predict the details of any legislation that may result from the Directive. It is, however, in line with and supportive of the increasing importance being attached by employers and employees to flexible working arrangements in the UK. Employers will be encouraged to take a positive approach to requests from employees, of either sex, to work part-time or as part of a job share arrangement. At present, if the employer turns down requests to work part-time or flexibly, this can in certain circumstances amount to indirect sex discrimination. Employers are allowed to argue that they are justified in their refusal, perhaps because of the seniority of the post and the need for continuity of service. They do need to be able to show this very clearly.

The Directive includes a number of proposals that would help create a climate in the workplace where part-time work is made more accessible. It states that employers should so far as possible give consideration to:

- requests by workers for transfers from full-time to part-time work; requests by workers for transfers from part-time work to full-time work, or to increase their working time, should the opportunity arise;

- the provision of timely information on the availability of part-time work and full-time positions in order to facilitate transfers from full-time to part-time work and vice versa;
- measures to facilitate access to part-time work at all levels of the enterprise, including skilled and managerial positions;
- measures to facilitate, where appropriate, access by part-time workers to vocational training to enhance career opportunities;
- the provision of appropriate information to existing bodies representing workers about part-time working in the organisation.

The Directive seeks to improve the employment conditions of part-time workers by stating that the pro rata principle should apply where appropriate.

At present EU law and UK law only address gender discrimination. When part-timers are paid lower wages they have to show they have been indirectly discriminated against on the grounds of sex. If payment of lower wages to part-timers was made unlawful, this could have a significant effect on the rights of part-timers.

9.4 Study leave

Provision for study leave should fall within staff development policies. Usually the studies are related to the employee's present, or possible future, work with the organisation.

Some organisations give time off with pay for studies related to an approved formal course or learning opportunity. The study time varies a few hours a week, one day a week or regular blocks of days. Time off in lieu may be agreed for an evening class which would be eligible for time off with pay if it were in the day time.

Other employers help with the fees but expect the work to be done out of working hours. The conditions of financial support for training may include a penalty clause, where the employee has to pay back some or all of the money if they leave before an agreed period of service after the course.

The *Green Book* advocates provision for training and development. Employees covered by it are entitled to paid leave of absence for the purpose of sitting approved examinations. In addition, leave may be granted for the purpose of final revision for approved examinations.

Many organisations make some provision for taking exams and revision. Some provide paid leave for formal study time, but few are able to provide secondments to full-time courses with pay.

Policy issues

Answers to the following questions will help to frame a policy:

- What values and principles, and which policies of the organisation, relate to this and how?
- Does the course or learning opportunity have to relate to the employee's present or future work in the organisation?
- What will the impact of time off be on both colleagues and users? Will we need to provide cover or will the service delivery be delayed?
- What will the benefit be to colleagues and to users of the learning or qualification?
- Will the policy include both paid and unpaid time off?
- Will the organisation be able to contribute to fees, and if so, in what circumstances?
- Will the right to study leave depend on a minimum number of years service?
- If we do make a financial contribution, will there be a penalty clause if the employee leaves within a certain time period? If an employer does want to insist that the money is repaid should the person leave before the end of the specified period, this must either be put in the contract of employment or the employee's written agreement obtained before the course is undertaken.

> **Example**
>
> Attendance at examinations is one circumstance in which special leave with or without pay of up to five days (pro rata for part-time staff) may be authorised by the National Director.

9.5 Unpaid leave

Leave which is unpaid, and in addition to the annual leave in the contract, may be taken a day at a time for special circumstances when annual leave has run out, or in a pre-planned block ranging from a few days to months.

Provision for unpaid leave has several benefits:

- Well trained, experienced employees are retained. They may otherwise be lost if they have to resign in order to take a trip away or do a full-time course.
- The employee comes back refreshed and remotivated.
- Another employee has the opportunity to act up for a fixed period.
- Unpaid leave from a post rather than a resignation may save the post from being cut.
- It gives an employee some space in which to plan to move from the organisation, where this is agreed to be beneficial to both parties.

However, at times an employee whom the employer does wish to retain decides to take the opportunity of the break to resign.

The costs will include some of the following:

- the cost of locum staff;
- delay in delivery of the work;
- added pressure on other staff.

The following questions may help in decision making:

- Does our Staff Development Policy give any guidance relevant to unpaid leave?
- How valuable is the member of staff in terms of their experience and level of skill?
- Are they likely to resign if refused?
- Are there options for managing the work during the period of absence?
- How often is this likely to happen with this employee and with others? Can we support this level of unpaid leave?
- Does it matter what the unpaid leave is for? Will we respond differently for example if it is for childcare two days a week for a year as opposed to a trip?

> **Examples**
>
> - Unpaid leave is usually discretionary and must be sought in advance.
>
> - Unpaid leave (in excess of contractual paid holiday) may be taken to coincide with school holidays for those who are responsible for children. Not more than ten working days may be taken in any one calendar year. Eight weeks notice of the days to be taken must be given to the director.
>
> - At the discretion of the director, in consultation with the chair, sympathetic consideration will be given to any request for unpaid leave of up to four weeks in excess of an employee's annual holiday entitlement.

(See also the section in Chapter 6 *Holidays/TOIL* on *Building up extra holiday time.*)

The 1997 IDS Study found that some companies offer unpaid longer term leave for looking after dependants, in the form of 'responsibility leave' or career breaks. For example, at Barclays Bank staff may take a responsibility break of between one and six months.

9.6 Sabbaticals

Sabbaticals are extra periods of leave, offered to staff who have long service records, typically five to ten years. A sabbatical is usually of an extended nature e.g. three to six months is in addition to annual holiday entitlement and is almost always paid.

The purposes can include:

- to give the employee a chance to try out something else, possibly with the aim of moving on, but with the safety net of a job to return to if needed;
- to reward experienced staff with the opportunity to do a project or activity unrelated to work, not normally possible given the time constraints;
- to benefit an employee's performance, by broadening their experience and leaving them refreshed and reinvigorated.

Some organisations do have a policy of offering sabbaticals, but this is not common.

Examples

- Sabbaticals are offered at the discretion of the director.

- After five years service, staff are entitled to elect for either sabbatical or extended leave. The sabbatical is six months leave on half pay or three months on full pay. The extended leave option gives five extra days annual leave per year after five years service and then one more for each year up to ten as a maximum.

- At the discretion of the director, in consultation with the chair, a period of between four weeks and one year may be taken as unpaid sabbatical leave, provided that not less than four months notice in writing is given by the employee.

- Sabbatical leave may be taken by staff who have a minimum of seven years service with the organisation. The leave will be for a maximum of six months, unpaid and at the discretion of the management. Only one sabbatical can be taken in any seven-year period. They can only be taken by one person per department or region in any one leave year. They must be timed to fit in with departmental needs and must be agreed with the head of department.

- Management staff have a paid sabbatical leave of four weeks after 15 years service.

- Some general managers and directors receive three months paid sabbatical leave every five years.

Chapter Ten

Making Financial Provision

Employing staff implies relatively predictable costs, not only for salaries and NI, but also for items such as:

- maternity pay;
- sick pay;
- locums recruited to provide cover;
- additional pay for staff who take on extra work to provide cover.

Statistics

Insurance companies have statistics that show the likelihood of sickness absence.

> 1.7 million people are currently off work for six months or longer...... According to Department of Social Security statistics, you are sixteen times more likely to be unable to work for more than six months than die before the age of 65.

quoted by Company A.

At April 12th 1995:

> 224,000 men and women had been unable to work for six months to one year; 583,000 from one to three years; 1,068,000 for over three years.

quoted by Company B, from Social Security Statistics, 1996. Table D1.05.

There are a number of implications of this:

- Figures from 1997 show the average absence rate (for all absences) is 3.59 per cent. Workload planning needs to take account of absence, if the organisation is to avoid staff struggling to meet unrealistic expectations (Industrial Society Report).
- The costs of maternity pay, sick pay and pay for cover need to be planned for through budgeting, reserves or insurance schemes.

These are the necessary safeguards of a prudent, well-managed organisation, which is not vulnerable to collapse when staff are absent.

This chapter looks at some of the methods for making financial provision, describes some examples from practice, and gives sources of further information.

10.1 What employers should do

Before deciding which of the financial option(s) to pursue, an employer needs to:

- understand the legal requirements for payment for maternity absence and
- sickness absence;
- discuss and decide on appropriate policies which take into account
  —the extent to which they want to be a good and fair employer,
  —the external environment,
  —the financial capacity of the organisation.

They are then in a position to manage absence with realistic financial plans.
The options include:

- budget provision;
- reserves;
- permanent health insurance, either:
—by the organisation or
—by individual members of staff;
- Key Worker Insurance;
- the Department of Social Security non-contributory and contributory benefits.

10.2 Legal framework

Employers' financial obligations to absent employees

Statute provides the basic obligations which most employers will add to through their contracts of employment. At present employers are obliged:

- To pay according to statute those who are taking time off under a statutory right, such as representatives of a recognised Trade Union (see Chapter 4).
- To pay staff for the annual holiday they are entitled to under their contracts of employment (see Chapter 6). Minimum paid annual holiday of three weeks (rising to four weeks in 1999) will also become a statutory right once the Working Time Directive is implemented in the UK, and is already a statutory right of employees in the public sector.
- To pay SSP to qualifying employees (see Chapter 5) and to make the payments during sickness absence that are provided for in the contract of employment.
- To pay employees in full during the statutory notice period if they are unable to work because of sickness. This obligation is contained in S88 of the ERA and is often overlooked by employers. The employee loses this right if he or she has a contractual right to notice that is at least one week longer than the statutory notice (see below).
- To pay SMP to eligible women employees, and to pay any additional contractual maternity pay and any other paid parental leave allowed for in the contract.
- To meet any other contractual obligations for paid absences such as carers' and compassionate leave.

  This list is not static and, as in all areas of the law affecting absence management, change occurs rapidly.

Example

Sickness payments during the notice period

> An employer dismisses two employees, **A** and **B**, because of prolonged sickness absence. Both of them are entitled to one month's notice under the contract of employment. **A** has been with the employer for over seven years, **B** for only two-and-a-half. The employer pays both of them SSP only during the notice period reasoning that both had by then exhausted the entitlement to contractual sick pay. This only allows for two weeks on full pay and two weeks on half pay regardless of length of service.

> Both employees take legal advice. **B** is told that because his contractual notice (one month) is more than a week longer than his statutory notice (one week), he has no statutory entitlement to full pay for that week of his statutory notice period.

> **A**, however, is advised that because she has a statutory notice period of seven weeks after seven complete years of service her contractual notice period is less than her statutory entitlement. She is therefore entitled to benefit from S88 of the ERA which gives her a right to full pay throughout the statutory notice period. The exhaustion of her contractual sick pay does not affect her statutory rights.

There is continuity of service while an employee is off sick, so long as the person has not resigned or been dismissed through incapacity to do the job or any other job in the organisation. If an employee has been dismissed because of sickness and is re-engaged within 26 weeks continuity is deemed to be preserved.

10.3 Budget provision

Once the organisation has its absence policies in place and knows its average absence rate per annum, it is able to budget to cover absence. There should be a line in the budget to cover the possible costs. Use of the contingency heading in the budget is another option, provided it is large enough to be able to cover absence as well as other possible contingencies, like bad debts or Industrial Tribunal costs.

Our findings showed a number of organisations who admitted they did not currently make such provision. The enquiry prompted them to think about these issues and to take action to address them.

Examples

A. One small voluntary arts organisation, with under ten staff, budgets ten per cent of staff costs each year to cover locum costs for absence. If this is, in the event, not needed, then it is used for special projects. The figure is £3,000–£6,000.

B. Another such organisation has a joint budget line for absence and for recruitment costs.

Our findings showed a number of organisations who admitted they did not currently make such provision. The enquiry prompted them to think about these issues and to take action to address them.

10.4 Reserves

Using reserves for such costs is another option. This option is open to companies limited by guarantee and to unincorporated associations. Registered charities need to pay attention to the guidance of the Charity Commissioners in relation to reserves. This is clearly set out in the leaflet CC19 'Charities' Reserves' available from any of their offices. Publication of material from the leaflet is not permissible without their authority (see Resource section for the contact details).

10.5 Permanent Health Insurance

There are a number of PHI policies offered by insurance companies. Employers must take independent financial advice. The information here is from a few policies given by way of example. Recommendations are not appropriate. The information from these companies in particular was included because of their assistance and willingness. Insurance taken out by the employer is a route which some medium to large organisations have taken and recommend.

The schemes described here are from two companies referred to as Company A and Company B. Both are commonly used by the voluntary sector. The policies operate within the same broad framework but with some important differences, such as the minimum premium.

Of the schemes on offer, three types are described below:

- Company schemes;
- Voluntary schemes;
- Schemes for individuals.

10.5.1 Taken out by the employer – company schemes

Purpose. The purpose of these policies is to provide cover in the event of accident or sickness occurring, which results in the incapacity for work of an insured person. The emphasis is on employer-paid insurances for the benefit of employees who suffer long term disability. Payment of benefit is to the employer, who, at their discretion, will pay the disabled employee as Part Salary Continuation. This payment will assist the employee to continue to meet their present financial commitments despite the incapacity for work.

The benefits of having a scheme. Company B argues that not only does PHI guarantee an income when employees need it most but also the removal of financial worries can aid recovery to health. Since guaranteed income protection is highly valued, it can also work to attract and retain staff.

Required legal status. There may be restrictions on eligibility for company schemes in terms of legal status. In the scheme of Company A, for example, the organisation must be a legal partnership or company and not an unincorporated body.

Non-Selection Limit (NSL). Most group PHI schemes benefit from a 'Non-Selection Limit' (NSL) facility. This is a specified maximum level of cover per employee up to which no evidence of health is required from participating employees. Inevitably the amount of cover in a non-selection scheme is lower.

If the level of cover does exceed the NSL, then the member of the scheme (employee) will need to provide details of health.

Company A's scheme requires a declaration if any employee is incapacitated on or during the two months preceding the cover date. This will mean that for new employees joining the scheme the employer will need to have made enquiries regarding the health of the employee before engaging them (see Chapter 5 Section 5.1.3).

Company B requires new employees to join the scheme at the first opportunity they are 'actively at work'. This means they should be in their normal full-time occupation on the date on which they first become eligible without having been absent for the first two months.

There may be a number of qualifying criteria before a scheme is accepted for non-selection. Company B has a minimum of five lives and Company A has several criteria for non-selection schemes.

Exclusions. Some specified conditions are excluded from most policies including any incapacity to do with HIV and AIDS. This is common to the policies and one company stated in the literature that they regretted this exclusion but they would be unable to offer the policy at all, if it was inclusive.

The process. The organisation decides:

- which employees will be eligible for the company PHI scheme – it can be all or one or more categories;
- how soon after the start of an employee's illness the PHI income should begin; (this is called a deferred period. The choices are usually 13, 26 or 52 weeks. For larger schemes 28 weeks may be offered.)

- the age to which benefits will continue to be paid;
- the level of benefits to be made available to the employees;
- whether to take the option of inflation related benefits, if available.

The costs. The cost of the scheme depends on a number of variables, which may include:

- the level of benefits;
- the deferred period before PHI income starts;
- the number, age and sex of the members;
- the cessation age(s) set up for the scheme;
- the members' occupations and location of employment;
- the claims history;
- whether there is cover for employers' pension premium contributions and NI contributions.

The organisation has to provide a proposal including all the required information. The insurer then works out a premium for that organisation.

The minimum premium of Company A at the time of writing is £500 per annum. A minimum of three lives must be insured. A maximum of 100 lives is usually set, which means it is not suitable for large employers.

Company B have a minimum premium for small organisations of £1,450 from 1 October, 1996, which is reviewed annually. Five lives to be insured is their minimum for a non-selection scheme.

The financial benefits. The Inland Revenue set a maximum limit of 75 per cent of earnings for financial benefits from PHI schemes. PHI income is not taxable for the first two years of payment. Tax liability kicks in in the third year. The maximum of 75 per cent is based on the principle that people should not be better off not working.

Each scheme may also have limitations of benefit to a maximum set by the company offering it. For example, the maximum benefit per member in one scheme is £7,500 per month or £90,000 per annum.

The table below shows the maximum per cent of earnings which can be paid in another scheme.

Table I. – Maximum benefits		
Normal earnings per annum	**Percentage of normal earnings**	**Maximum total benefit per annum**
up to £45,000	75	£30,000
next £20,000 or part thereof	60	£42,000
next £95,000 or part thereof	40	£80,000

Some schemes offer two approaches to paying benefits:

Gross-pay approach: This is where the level of PHI income benefits are expressed as a proportion of gross normal earnings restricted to 75 per cent of gross normal earnings less a single person's long term Incapacity Benefit.

Fully-integrated approach: This is where it is the same as above but that the **total** amount of State Incapacity Benefit, including that for dependants etc. will be taken into account.

Two levels of benefit are payable in two different sets of circumstances.

Total benefit: Members of schemes are eligible for this benefit if immediately prior to incapacity the insured person was following a gainful occupation and after the onset of incapacity the insured person is not following any other gainful occupation.

Proportionate benefit: Eligibility for this benefit arises if immediately prior to incapacity the insured person was following a gainful occupation and as a result of the incapacity the insured person is following a gainful occupation other than their normal occupation or are following their normal occupation but part-time, in either case meaning a reduction in normal earnings.

Length of payment. Usually, payment will be made up to the date agreed for cessation in the scheme, so long as the member is prevented by illness or injury from working. Some schemes cease payment if the employee is dismissed on grounds of incapacity through ill-health, which can be a major disadvantage for employers and employees. This may no longer be an option for employers in the light of recent cases (see section on significant legal cases following).

Other schemes, subject to their policy conditions, arrange to continue payment of benefits direct to the member, should they cease to be an employee. It would be important to check this point with an insurer should you be considering a scheme.

Inflation protection. A degree of inflation protection is offered by some schemes.

Example of costs and benefits.
An organisation (Company A) in computer services insuring 40 lives.
Total salaries: £1,039,815.
Policy would provide income benefits of 75 per cent of salary, less the basic rate of state single person's long term Incapacity Benefit.
The premium in the first year would be £6,537.48* per annum or £572.03 per month.

Claiming benefits. Evidence of incapacity may be required in order to claim benefit.

- Company A require that the insured person is under the regular supervision and treatment of a medical practitioner in respect of incapacity.

- Company B reserves the right to have a claimant examined as required, at its own expense, by a Medical Officer appointed by them.

Significant cases. In relation to employers who provide permanent health insurance (PHI) schemes as part of employees' contractual entitlements (see below) there have been some highly significant recent decisions by the courts.

In effect the decisions mean that an employer cannot dismiss an employee for long term sickness absence where there is a PHI scheme in place, unless the employee has committed an act of gross misconduct.

Recent Cases

In *Aspden* v. *Webbs Poultry and Meat Group (Holdings) Ltd* (1996) IRLR 521, Mr Aspden was covered by a PHI scheme. The High Court held that there was an implied term in his contract that he would not be dismissed by his employer in such a way that he lost his right to benefit under the scheme, unless he himself had fundamentally breached the employment contract.

In *Brompton* v. *AOC International Ltd and UNUM Ltd* (1997) IRLR 639, Mr Brompton was receiving payments under AOCI's PHI scheme and had not worked for his employer since 1982. AOCI's insurers discovered in 1989 that he was doing some work in his wife's shop and some occasional electrical jobs. The insurers decided that this breached the terms of the scheme and AOCI stopped payments to Mr Brompton ,who found short term work elsewhere. However, he then brought a claim for benefits under the PHI scheme which he said should have been paid after 1989. The company conceded that it should not have stopped paying him but argued that Mr Brompton had brought the contract to an end by finding other work. The Court of Appeal

---

*premium correct at the time of writing

disagreed and said that Mr Brompton was entitled to benefits under the scheme until his death in 1995 and had not terminated his contract by finding other work. The Court also said that AOCI probably would not have been entitled to terminate the contract either because of the existence of an implied term as in Mr Aspden's case.

In a Scottish case Court of Session [*Adin* v. *Sedco Forex International Resources Ltd* (1997) IRLR 280], the Court said that the employers were not entitled to defeat an employee's rights to short and long term disability benefits by dismissing him. In this case the rights were expressly set out in the contract and there was no need for the employee to rely on an implied term.

In another case [*Bainbridge* v. *Circuit Foil UK Ltd* (1997) IRLR 305] the company stopped the PHI scheme altogether – which the rules of the scheme allowed. However, they did not tell Mr Bainbridge what they were doing ; he simply found that his payments had stopped. The Court of Appeal said that, until the company told the employee that his contract had been varied by the ending of PHI, it was still liable under its contract with him to continue to make payments of sickness benefits provided for under the scheme. This was the case even though the company itself was no longer receiving the money from its insurers because it had brought the scheme to an end.

What employers should do. Taken together the cases quoted in the examples should encourage employers to think carefully about the commitment they are entering into with a PHI scheme. They should be aware that they are entering into contractual commitments to their employees which they cannot simply terminate at will.

The position is complex because employers who adopt PHI schemes have two sets of contractual commitments running in parallel; their existing obligations under the contract of employment, and new obligations to the insurance company under the PHI contract. The two contracts may sometimes come into conflict but it is a mistake for an employer to think that the contract with the insurance company takes precedence over, or can extinguish, the employee's rights.

The cases also suggest that the handling of long term sickness absence must be different in a workplace with a PHI scheme. Employers will be anxious to comply with the insurance company's requirements and the insurers will want to conduct their own enquiries into the health of an employee who is applying for benefits. This does not mean that employers should forget about consulting with the employee or considering suitable alternative employment. The insurance company is also likely to consider all the alternatives before agreeing to pay out.

What is clear is that, where there is a PHI scheme, termination of the contract for reasons of prolonged sickness absence will only be an option in exceptional circumstances.

10.5.2 Taken out by employees as a group – voluntary schemes

These are for organisations, associations or companies, who are not able to fund a group protection scheme, but are keen to promote the benefits of income protection. The purpose of seeking income protection as a group is to obtain better terms. The terms offered will depend on the membership size, the type of business and the likely take-up rate. This is a very good option for employees where the employer is unable to offer any sort of a scheme because the terms will be considerably better than an individual scheme.

10.5.3 Taken out by employees as individuals – individual schemes

These are individual income protection plans or permanent health insurance schemes (PHIs).

Employers' role. Where the employer knows the limits of the organisational provision in the event of serious illness or accident, they may decide to give employees information about a range of PHI schemes. The employees are then in a position to make an informed choice about the level of protection they wish to secure for themselves, were they to be incapacitated from work. This may be particularly valuable to employees coming from a local authority scheme to a voluntary organisation, where the provision is much less than they are used to.

Purpose. PHI schemes aim to reduce the financial shock to an individual (and their family) should they be incapacitated for work for any length of time. Where people have fixed financial commitments dependent on their income from work, which will not be covered by the state benefits to which they are entitled, and it is either not feasible or not desirable to reduce them, then these policies might be of interest.

Company A offers an income protection plan 'which provides a regular tax free income should illness or accident prevent you from working. It is designed to help you maintain your standard of living until you are able to return to work.'

Limits to the benefits. Company A's policy allows you to insure up to 60 per cent of your regular gross annual earnings to a maximum annual income of £90,000. Other providers offer different maximum benefit limits. The payments may or may not be linked to the Retail Price Index. Some schemes include this provision, offering it as an option at additional cost.

Required employment status. You do not have to be in work to take out some PHI policies.

Company A's policy offers:

'Cover is available for people who work full-time, part-time up to 20 hours a week, unemployed for at least three months, or a houseperson. Cover is available for the latter two categories up to a maximum benefit of £10,000 per annum.'

Medical requirements. The schemes are likely to require evidence of incapacity. The Company A Scheme says 'To be eligible for benefit you must be under the regular supervision and treatment of a Medical Practitioner in respect of Incapacity.'

Example of costs and benefits. A 35-year-old male non-smoker who works as a computer operator/ programmer on a salary of £30,000. Initial benefit is £1500 per month after 26 consecutive weeks incapacity. The cover will continue up to his 60th birthday. The monthly premium would be £22.05.*

10.6 Key worker schemes

These are schemes whereby an employer insures for loss of a key employee through accident, illness or other absence. They may do this because they are heavily dependant on a particular person for the survival and running of the organisation and it is expensive to replace them on a temporary basis.

10.7 The National Insurance Scheme—injury and ill-health at work

Benefits are either contributory (i.e. available to claimants who meet the National Insurance contribution conditions) or non-contributory (i.e. available to anyone meeting the specific criteria of entitlement to a benefit).

The only contributory benefit in the context of sickness absence is Incapacity Benefit (formerly Invalidity Benefit). The principal non-contributory benefit is Severe Disablement Allowance. In addition, Industrial Injuries Benefits are payable to claimants who suffer disability as a result of accident or disease caused by their work (although, technically non-contributory, most claimants will have made contributions at some stage in their lives). The main Industrial Injuries Benefit is Disablement Benefit. Increases are payable in the form of Constant Attendance Allowance and Exceptionally Severe Disablement Allowance. Claimants who suffered accidents or onset of disease before 1 October 1990, may also be able to claim Reduced Earnings Allowance.

Payment of these benefits is unconnected to any claim for compensation for injury at work, although the Benefits Agency is entitled to make a recovery of benefits paid out on settlements of compensation, often many years later.

10.8 What employers should do

Every organisation, even very small ones, needs to assume they could have at least one long absence due to sickness or accident in any one year. They must plan and prepare for this. Larger organisations are even more likely to face significant absences, but also have potentially more resources with which to manage the situation.

---

*premium correct at the time of writing

Resources

WRITTEN RESOURCES

Books

The main books on employment law and personnel aimed at the voluntary sector are the following:

Individual authors

Sandy Adirondack
Just About Managing, 3rd ed LVSC, 1998, £14.95, 1-872582 80 X
Voluntary Sector Legal Handbook, with James Sinclair Taylor DSC, 1997, £35.00, 1-873869 79

Gill Taylor
Equal Opportunities: A Practical Handbook, Industrial Society, 1994, £19.95
Managing People, with Christine Thornton, DSC, 1995, £9.95, 1-873869 47 1
Managing Recruitment and Selection, DSC, 1996, £10.95, 1-873860 85 4
Managing Discipline and Dismissal, DSC, Forthcoming

Other Authors

Voluntary But Not Amateur, Forbes, Hayes and Reason, 5th ed, LVSC, 1998, £14.95, 1-872582 22 2
Getting Organised, Shirley Otto and Christine Holloway, Bedford Square Press, 1985.
Meeting the Stress Challenge, Neil Thornton, Michael Murphy and Steve Standing with Paul O'Neill. Wirobound A4 Manual, Russell House Publishing, 1997, £19.95. Tel 01297 443 948, 1-898924-902

ACAS

Produces a whole range of useful booklets and information most at £2.00 each. For example:
Discipline at Work
Employment Handbook
Absence and Labour Turnover
Hours of Work
Health and Employment
Full set of booklets £25.50
List of ACAS publications can be obtained from ACAS Reader Ltd, PO Box 16, Earl Shilton, Leicester, LE9 8ZZ. Tel 0116 852 225

Charity Commissioners

The Charity Commissioners produce leaflets and small booklets on setting up and running a charity. St Alban's House, 57–60 Haymarket, London, SW1Y 4Q. Tel 00171 210 4477

Child Poverty Action Group

Rights Guide to Non-Means-Tested-Benefits, 20th ed, 1997/8 £8.95, produced annually

Department of Social Security

Statutory Sick Pay Manual for Employers (NI270) and supplement
Statutory Sick Pay Check Your Rights (NI244)

Health and Safety Executive (HSE)
Mental Wellbeing in the Workplace. A resource pack for management training and development. Produced by Cranfield School of Management for the Government Inter-Agency Group, £25.00, order 01787 881 165

HMSO
Codes of Practice Under the DDA, PO Box 276, London, SW8 5DT

Incomes Data Services
An independent research organisation providing information and analysis on pay conditions, pensions, employment law and personnel and policy practice in the UK and the rest of Europe, including the bi-monthly IDS brief on developments in employment law. Produced a study on *Managing Absence* in March, 1998 (Study 645).

Institute of Personnel and Development
From Absence to Attendance, Evans Alistair and Palmer Steve, 1998, £17.95 (discount for IPD members). The IPD publishes many other books and reports covering the whole range of training, personnel and development topics.

Industrial Society
Publishes many books/videos and CD-roms relevant to HR/personnel/employment law, for example:
Harassment in the Workplace, information pack, £50
Danger! Sex at Work, Nonni Williams, £9.99
Harassment, Bullying and Violence at Work, Sonia Arnold and Angela Ishmael, £12.95
Equal Opportunities, The Manager's Handbook, Gill Taylor, £19.95
The New Employment Contract, Pat Leighton and Aidan O'Donnell, £14.99
A Guide to the Employments Acts, Joan Henderson, £14.99
Unfair Dismissal, Richard Painter, £12.95
The Work Environment, Patricia Leighton, £12.95
Statutory Maternity Pay and Maternity Rights, Sue Morris, £12.95
Industrial Tribunals, Phillip Parry, £12.95
Maternity, Paternity and Adoption Leave Information Pack, £50

Legal Action Group
Employment Law and Advisor's Handbook, LAG, 1996, £19.00
Employment Tribunal Procedure, LAG, 1996, £22.00
Maternity Rights, LAG, £15.00

National Council for Voluntary Organisations (NCVO)
The Good Employment Guide for the Voluntary Sector, NCVO, 1997, £30.00
Plus other information and books relevant for voluntary sector managers. Phone for latest publications list, 0171 713 6161

MIND – the mental health charity
Positive About Mental Health: Ten Tips for Employers. A pack on mental health and employment, 1998

Journals/magazines

Institute of Personnel and Development
People Management, fortnightly. Free to IPD members. Also available on subscription.

Industrial Relations Service
Equal Opportunities Review is published bi-monthly. Gives news on discrimination law updates and case law. Publishes statistics and new items. £80 per annum subscription.
Management Review reports on issues of interest to managers. Very glossy and absolutely the last word on in-depth reviews of personnel management issues. £105 per copy.

Labour Research Department
Labour Research monthly magazine mainly for the trade union movement. Covers updates in EU and employment law.

Web pages

Institute of Personnel and Development
Is on the web at http://www.ipd.co.uk

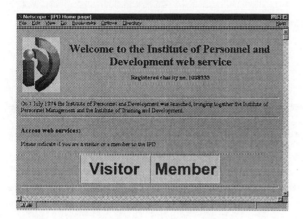

Libraries

Institute of Personnel and Development
The IPD Library has the most comprehensive collection of personnel, training and development reference material in Europe. Service is free to members. They publish a list of information notes on various topics of interest such as sexual harassment, Aids and the workplace, counselling etc..

London Voluntary Service Council
Resource centre has a limited selection of personnel and legal reference books.

Industrial Society
The library contains more than 25,000 personnel documents drawing on best practices, polices and procedures of members organisations.

Employment reference guides

Croner's Reference Guides
Croner's publish 14 different publications with a quarterly updating service as the law changes on Employment Law, and 23 on Health and Safety. For example: (prices are approximate.)

Employment Law	£320
Discrimination Law	£150
Personnel Forms and Procedures	£330
Managing a Voluntary Organisation	£155

Price quoted is the approximate initial purchase price; there is also an annual updating service fee. Croner's also produce booklets on key issues such as Discipline and Grievance, Health and Safety.

Gee Publishing
Gee produce 17 personnel and employment resources, and a further nine on payroll and a wide range on other business topics. Most of these include updates between two and six times a year, plus

sometimes newsletters on the topic. Some relate to specific industries. Some examples (with the annual charge) are:

Essential Facts: Employment	£50.00
	£125 (with helpline and newsletter)
The Personnel Manager's Factbook	£125
Employment Letters and Procedures	£80
Part-time, Temporary and Casual Employment Handbook	£115
Health and Safety Lawbase	£500 (computer software only)

Incomes Data Services
Produces bi-monthly IDS brief on developments in employment law.

Advice lines

ACAS
Each regional office will give free advice on issues to do with employee relations, disciplinary matters and Industrial Tribunals.

Charity Commissioners
The Charity Commissioners will give advice on all legal aspects of setting up a charity, restructuring and changing charitable objects.

Croner's Law Line
This service includes the telephone advisory service, *Personnel in Practice* reference book, disk version of the reference book of your choice, *Employment Digest* (eight page fortnightly newsletter), *Employment Case Digest* (eight page monthly newsletter). The subscription of £721.44 allows as much access to an advisor as you want.

GEE's Help Line
An optional extra which can be purchased by subscribers to *Essential Facts: Employment.*

Industrial Society
Employment Law Helpline. This is a perk of membership. A team of six advisers giving advice on UK/ EU employment law and personnel procedures to best management practices. Takes 11,000 calls per year.

Institute of Personnel and Development (IPD)
A free advice line for members (in most cases membership is by examination). A legal advisory service for members, related to their professional activities. The service offers a quick check as to the legal implications of issues arising in their work. It is not able to offer in-depth advice on complex issues.

Interchange Training
Offer an advice line on all legal issues for voluntary organisations. Initial one hour's consultation is free; after that it is charged at affordable subsidised rates. One year's after advice follow up is free.

They also offer personalised seminars for a group on legal issues. £50 for 2–3 hours on the issues of the group's choice.

MIND — The mental health charity
MIND InfoLine provides information and advice on mental health issues such as situations of distress of an employee. They also provide access to books and articles including ones from the US.

National Council for Voluntary Organisations (NCVO)
The NCVO voluntary sector helpdesk is a free advice and information line for people in the voluntary sectors. It covers a range of issues including human resource management.

Contact details of agencies providing relevant resources

ACAS
Brandon House
180 Borough High St
London SE1 1LW   0171 210 3000

ACAS reader
PO Box 16
Earl Shilton
Leicester LE9 8ZZ   0145 852 225

Distributes all the ACAS leaflets

Apex Trust
St Alphage House, Wingate Annex
2 Fore St
London EC2Y 5DA   0171 638 5931

Advice on ex-offenders' employment rights

Centre for Accessible Environments
Nutmeg House
60 Gainsford St
London SE1 2NY   0171 357 8182

Charity Commissioners
St Alban's House
57–60 Haymarket
London SW1Y 4QX   0171 210 4477

City Centre
32–35 Featherstone St
London EC1Y 8QX   0171 608 1338

Leaflets, books and advice on employment practices, mainly to individuals working in the City

Child Poverty Action Group
Publications Department
94 White Lion St
London N1   0171 837 3676

Commission for Racial Equality
Elliot House
10–12 Allington St
London SW1E 5EH   0171 828 7022

Croner Publications
Croner House
London Road
Kingston-upon-Thames
Surrey KT2 6SR   0181 547 3333

Department of Social Security
Look up the local address in the phone book

Department of Trade and Industry
Leaflet Distribution Unit
Camberton Ltd, Unit 8
Goldthorpe Industrial Estate
Rotherham S63 9BL   01709 888 688

Disability Alliance
1st floor East, Universal House
88–94 Wentworth St
London E1 7SA   0171 247 8776
Campaigns for better employment and benefit rights for people with disabilities.

Disability Awareness in Action
11 Belgrave Rd
London SW1V 1RB   0171 834 0477
DAA is a collaborative project between Disabled Peoples International, Impact, Inclusion International and the World Federation for the Deaf

Disabled Living Foundation
380–384 Harrow Rd
London W9 2HG   0171 289 6111
Provides information on employing people with disabilities and accessibility information

DIAL UK
Park Lodge
St Catherine's Hospital
Tickhill Rd
Balby
Doncaster DN4 8QN   01302 310 123

Directory of Social Change
24 Stephenson Way
London NW1 2DP   0171 209 4949

Employers' Forum on Disability
Nutmeg House
60 Gainsford St
London SE1 2NY   Tel/Minicom   0171 403 3020

Equal Opportunities Commission
Overseas House,
Quay St
Manchester M3 3HN   0161 833 9244

Federation of Independent Advice Centres
4 Dean's Court
St Paul's Churchyard
London EC4U 5AA   0171 2489 1800

GEE & Company
100 Avenue Rd
Swiss Cottage
London NW3 3PG
           Customer Services   0171 393 7400
Provides an information service and journals that are updated quarterly on employment issues

Health and Safety Executive
Book Department
PO Box 1999
Sudbury
Suffolk CO10 6FS   0178 788 1165

Incomes Data Services
77 Bastwick St
London EC1B 3TT   0171 324 2599
Research organisation providing information on employment law and personnel practices

Independent Theatre Council
12 The Leathermarket
Weston St
London SE1 3ER   0171 403 1727

Industrial Relations Service
18–20 Highbury Place
London N5 1QP   0171 354 5858
Publishes journals and other information on employment and equalities issues

Industrial Society
Robert Hyde House
48 Bryanston Square
London W1H 7LN   0171 262 2401
Runs training courses, an employment law helpline and publishes reports on voluntary sector and employment issues

Institute of Personnel and Development
IPD House
35 Camp Rd
Wimbledon
London SW19 4UX   0181 971 9000

Interchange Trust
Interchange Studios
Dalby St
London NW5 3NQ   0171 267 9421

LAGER
Unit 1G Leroy House
436 Essex Rd
London N1 3QP   Gay men 0171 704 6066
                       Lesbians 0171 704 8066
Regular bulletins on lesbian and gay employment rights and issues and can give advice to individuals

London Hazards Centre
Interchange Studios
Dalby St
London NW5 2NQ   0171 267 3387
Runs training courses and publishes materials on health and safety issues

London Voluntary Service Council
356 Holloway Rd
London N7 6PA   0171 700 8107

Management Development Network
39 Gabriel House
Odessa St
London SE16 1HQ   0171 232 0726
Directory of management consultants who specialise in working with the voluntary sector

Maternity Alliance
45 Beech St
London EC2P 2LX   0171 588 8582
Campaigns for better maternity rights for all women, advice line, training courses

MIND – The mental health charity
15–19 Broadway
London E15 4BB   0181 519 2122
          InfoLine London   0181 522 1728
          outside London   0345 660 163

National Association of Councils for Voluntary Service
3rd Floor, Arundel Court
177 Arundel St
Sheffield S1 2NU   0114 278 6636

National Centre for Volunteering
Regent's Wharf
8 All Saints St
London N1 9RL   0171 388 9888
Leaflets and advice on working with volunteers

NACRO
169 Clapham Rd
London SW9 0PU   0171 582 6500
Advice on ex-offenders' employment rights

National Council for Voluntary Organisations (NCVO)
Regent's Wharf
8 All Saints St
London N1 9RL   0171 713 6300
          Helpline   0845 600 4500

National Disability Council
Disability Unit
Room 6–11, The Adelphi
1–11 John Adam St
London WC2N 6HT
The new body set up by the Disability Discrimination Act

New Ways to Work
309 Upper St
London N1 2TY   0171 226 4026
                    0171 388 9888
Produce publications and campaigning on job sharing and other forms of flexible working

Sinclair Taylor & Martin, Solicitors
9 Thorpe Close, Portobello Rd
London W10 5XL   0181 969 3667
Specialists in employment law and other aspects of law applicable to charities

NORTHERN COLLEGE LIBRARY
95233   BARNSLEY S75 3ET